The End-of-Life Handbook *b*
This book explains in clear, nor
and what to do to help them an
dying, keep this book handy and follow its sound advice.

> —David Spiegel, MD, Willson Professor and associate
> chair of the Department of Psychiatry and Behavioral
> Sciences at the Stanford University School of Medicine,
> author of *Living Beyond Limits,* and coauthor of *Group
> Therapy for Cancer Patients*

The End-of-Life Handbook *illumines the opacity which cloaks life's final
chapter. Acknowledging the universal fear of the unknown, Feldman and
Lasher light the trail which leads patients and families to reconciliation with
life's last challenge.*

> —Walter M. Bortz II, MD, clinical associate professor of
> medicine at the Stanford University School of Medicine
> and author of *We Live Too Short and Die Too Long, Dare
> to Be 100,* and *Living Longer for Dummies*

The End-of-Life Handbook *is a rich practical guide for meeting the medical,
social, and emotional challenges that accompany the serious illness of a loved
one. Feldman and Lasher's wise and sensitive suggestions make this book
required reading for everyone negotiating life's most intimate passage.*

> —Dale G. Larson, Ph.D., author of *The Helper's Journey*

*This book shines a light into the dark forest of dying. It's all here—how we
tend to feel, what we might want to say (or not), how to deal with doctors and
diagnoses, how to come to terms with our own soul's desires. The book is a
down-to-earth distillation of the wisdom and experience we need to care for
someone we love at the end of life and to care for ourselves.*

> —Brad Stuart MD, Senior Medical Director of the S
> Visiting Nurse Association and Hospice

This is a practical road map for finding a way through the challenges of caregiving, illness, and loss. Anyone who has questions will find useful information and helpful recommendations here.

> —Marcia Lattanzi Licht, MA, RN, LPC, cofounder of HospiceCare in Boulder, CO, educator, psychotherapist, and author of *The Hospice Choice*

Acknowledging a diagnosis of a terminal illness and recognizing that difficult choices and different approaches to a love one's care may be necessary are enormous hurdles for most people. Confusing medical information, frightening hospital routines and widespread misconceptions in our culture add to families' burdens. The End of Life Handbook offers refreshing clarity to anyone confronting a loved one's terminal illness, breaking down the basic issues and medical jargon in easy-to-read language. Most importantly, it reminds caregivers that a "soft landing" is possible for their loved one and that they can still count their blessings, despite the difficult straits they are negotiating.

> —Larry Beresford, author of *The Hospice Handbook* and consulting writer with the National Hospice and Palliative Care Organization and Center to Advance Palliative Care

This publication is truly the first of its kind. Feldman and Lasher have reached out to families and caregivers to provide a comprehensive guide to the care of a loved one with a terminal illness. It answers every question of need with emphasis on the physical, emotional, and medical issues that encompass this most complicated and stressful phase of life.

> —Jules Sherman, DO, board-certified specialist in medical oncology and palliative medicine and chief medical officer of the Hospice of Dayton

The End-of-Life Handbook

A Compassionate Guide to Connecting with and Caring for a Dying Loved One

DAVID B. FELDMAN, PH.D.
S. ANDREW LASHER, JR., MD

New Harbinger Publications, Inc.

Publisher's Note

Care has been taken to confirm the accuracy of the information presented and to describe generally accepted practices. However, the authors, editors, and publisher are not responsible for errors or omissions or for any consequences from application of the information in this book and make no warranty, express or implied, with respect to the contents of the publication.

The authors, editors, and publisher have exerted every effort to ensure that any drug selection and dosage set forth in this text are in accordance with current recommendations and practice at the time of publication. However, in view of ongoing research, changes in government regulations, and the constant flow of information relating to drug therapy and drug reactions, the reader is urged to check the package insert for each drug for any change in indications and dosage and for added warnings and precautions. This is particularly important when the recommended agent is a new or infrequently employed drug.

Some drugs and medical devices presented in this publication may have Food and Drug Administration (FDA) clearance for limited use in restricted research settings. It is the responsibility of the health care provider to ascertain the FDA status of each drug or device planned for use in their clinical practice.

Distributed in Canada by Raincoast Books

Copyright © 2007 by David B. Feldman and S. Andrew Lasher, Jr.
New Harbinger Publications, Inc.
5674 Shattuck Avenue
Oakland, CA 94609
www.newharbinger.com

Cover and text design by Amy Shoup; Acquired by Tesilya Hanauer; Edited by Jasmine Star

All Rights Reserved. Printed in the United States of America.

Library of Congress CataloginginPublication Data

Feldman, David B.
  The end of life handbook : a compassionate guide to connecting with and caring for a dying loved one / David B. Feldman & Stephen Andrew Lasher Jr. ; foreword by Ira Byock.

    p. cm.
  Includes bibliographical references.
  ISBN13: 9781572245112 (pbk. : alk. paper)
  ISBN10: 1572245115 (pbk. : alk. paper)
  1. Palliative treatmentHandbooks, manuals, etc. 2. Terminally illFamily relationshipsHandbooks, manual, etc. 3. Terminal carePsychological aspectsHandbooks, manuals, etc. I. Lasher, Stephen Andrew. II. Title.

R726.8.F464 2007
616'.029dc22

                                    2007036683

09   08   07

10   9   8   7   6   5   4   3   2   1   First printing

Contents

Foreword

Caring for a person as he or she is dying is one of the most difficult yet important things we will ever do for someone we love. Most of us come to the task woefully ill prepared. Growing up in the United States, we have to a greater or lesser extent absorbed the orientation toward illness, aging, and dying of contemporary Western culture, summed up succinctly as "I don't want to think about it."

All our lives we've thought there is nothing worse than dying. But unfortunately there is. One thing worse than dying is dying badly. It's not just our own death we fear. We can't imagine anything worse than someone we love becoming ill and dying. But again, worse things can occur. More dreaded than losing people you love is knowing that they suffered as they died or, worse still, realizing that their suffering could have been prevented.

People rightly want to focus on life and living. Even when a person becomes ill, talking about dying can feel like giving up on life. The problem with unwavering avoidance of dying and death is that it keeps us from planning. As a consequence, most of us are utterly unprepared when this inevitable and inarguably important part of our lives happens.

I often talk to patients and families, as well as public groups, about advance directives—living wills and the durable power of attorney for health care. Frequently, the initial response from people is that they are not ready to discuss it. "I'm just not there yet, doctor," or "Do you think things are that far along?" I explain that every adult should have an advance directive; I have one, and so does everyone in my family, including my daughters in their twenties. It's hard for me to imagine anything worse than one of my daughters being seriously injured or ill, but if tragedy strikes our family, I want to keep it within our family. The cases that have shaped American law on end-of-life medical decisions—Karen Ann Quinlan, Nancy Cruzan, Terri Schiavo—were all young women.

Like it or not, when the day comes that we have lost the capacity to speak for ourselves, someone we know and trust will be called on to speak for us. While we can't alter the inherent vulnerability and frailty of being human, we can project our personal values and choices forward. By being proactive, we can not only protect our choices but also diminish the burden of decision making that our friends and family feel. That's why I have an advance directive. Otherwise, we make the hard job that our families will have even harder.

As awkward and anxiety provoking as it may be to contemplate illness and dying, preparing is essential. The cold truth is that about 80 percent of us will be physically dependent on others during the last months, weeks, or days of life. We will need help with basic daily activities, including the biological needs of eating, personal hygiene, and elimination. As we were when we were infants and toddlers, so we will be at the end of our life. If all that seems undignified, I suggest, it is merely human. Some species are born fully independent and die suddenly. Babies are utterly dependent on others for the first few months and remain reliant on their families and communities for basic needs and protection through childhood. The process is reversed at the far end of life, whether occasioned by age or by disease. Correspondingly, people have cared for their young, old, and frail since the beginning of our species; it's part of what makes us human.

Hospice and palliative care have made huge strides in changing the way people are cared for as they die. Even today, however, over half of deaths occur in hospitals. Nearly 20 percent of Americans end their days in intensive care units, often tethered to beds to keep them from dislodging IVs or breathing tubes. Dying is hard enough—it doesn't have to be *this* hard.

One would think that the general cultural avoidance of dying and death would dissolve at the doors of the medical center. Not true. In the mid-twentieth century, a dazzling string of advances in surgery, cardiology, the treatment of infections, and the understanding of disease made it seem that aging and death might one day be conquered. As a result, the topics of death and dying became taboo in the medical community. More recently, medical culture has begun to accept and integrate the fact that people eventually die. Still, the old observation that death feels like a failure to doctors remains true. Doctors care deeply about the people who are their patients, but they have been trained from day one to protect people from death. Medical education is focused on evidence-based treatments of disease. While this has resulted in notable successes in treating specific diseases, it has fostered a mechanistic, fix-it approach to patient care.

People are more than elegant machines. An exclusive focus on physiology ignores the emotional, social, and spiritual parts of a person's life. The fix-it mentality is also ultimately lacking, because at some point, despite cutting-edge treatments, everyone dies. When a person develops a life-threatening condition, he or she needs access to the very best treatments and medical centers. The person needs doctors and nurses trained not only in curing diseases but in caring for the people who have them. Yet even with the best doctors and nurses, people can feel bewildered and lost in the world of illness and in the complex, technical world of medical treatment.

Receiving a diagnosis of a terminal illness is a bit like stepping into a raft on a river with class IV rapids. Things abruptly begin moving too fast; people describe feeling unsteady, never fully in control. They are aware that unseen dangers may await them at every turn. People who are seriously ill—and those caring for someone who is ill—urgently need a guide who has run rivers like this before. A knowledgeable guide can help an ill person—and the family members also in the raft—to navigate these swift, rough, and foreboding waters. An experienced guide can alert people to the decisions that lie ahead and provide tips from people who've journeyed this way before, both mistakes to avoid and things you don't want to miss. A guide through illness can point out snags lying beneath the surface of the health care system, such as sometimes perverse financial reimbursement incentives, or forces of groupthink and assumptions about the way things are done that can sweep people away in a direction they would never have chosen.

An adept guide would never presume to plan for a journeyer, but would know the questions to ask so that the traveler could carefully choose his or her own path. The ideal guide would be part doctor, whose counseling is rooted in medical expertise, and part psychologist, who could explore and assist with sources of personal distress, helping to maximize the individual's and family's personal well-being.

In this handbook, David B. Feldman, a clinical psychologist, and S. Andrew Lasher Jr., a palliative care physician, with many combined years of experience caring for people with advanced illness, extend to reluctant travelers critical information, suggest essential questions to ask, and offer sound counsel for the journey through illness, the frailty of advanced age, and the challenge of caregiving. It would be ideal if they could climb into the raft with you. But the next best thing is to pack the book you have in your hand. Hold on to it during the journey ahead.

> —Ira Byock, M.D.
> author of *Dying Well* and *The Four Things That Matter Most*
> Lebanon, New Hampshire
> August 2007

Acknowledgments

As this book was written with families in mind, it goes without saying that we would like to acknowledge our own families—in particular our parents—for their unending love and support. Without their presence, we never could have become empathic, enabled professionals. We never could have thrived in this rewarding field of practice, and certainly never could have written this book.

We also wish to thank the staff of the Veterans Affairs Palo Alto Hospice and Palliative Care Center. These sensational physicians, nurses, psychologists, social workers, chaplains, nurse assistants, and support staff have created a near-perfect atmosphere for the veterans who receive their expert assistance. And it is these noble veterans whom we would like to thank the most. Having served their country in both war and peace, having endured suffering and alienation, joy and elation, they graciously allowed us to view the final acts of their lives. In placing themselves in our care, they have afforded us the opportunity to grow as professionals and as people. We owe them a debt of gratitude we could never repay. We hope we served them well.

Introduction

You're probably reading these words because someone you love is facing a life-threatening or terminal illness. Maybe your loved one has been diagnosed with cancer, heart failure, Alzheimer's disease, lung disease, or any number of other serious conditions. Perhaps he or she has struggled with this illness for many years, or maybe the news came with little warning. Whatever the circumstances, it's natural to feel unprepared or even overwhelmed.

Most of us never expect to face issues like these. Only a few decades ago, the end of life looked quite different than it does today. People died of accidents or severe diseases relatively soon after they occurred. They went through life unconcerned with its end, assuming that they would die quickly and relatively painlessly of "old age." Since then, however, advanced technology has afforded people the opportunity to live with severe medical conditions for greater periods of time than ever before.

People may be told that they have a life-threatening illness a year or more in advance of passing away.

As a side effect of this situation, you and your loved one face unprecedented choices about how and where the death will occur. You may confront numerous medical opinions and struggle with how to decide among them. More fundamentally, you may wonder how to speak with your loved one about these crucial choices without adding to his or her emotional burden. Given such difficult issues, you also may be riding your own emotional roller coaster. Fear, sadness, anger, grief, hope, and love—these are just some of the feelings people experience as they come to grips with a loved one's serious illness.

We've sat at the bedsides of many patients, helping them and their families navigate these difficult choices and the emotional turmoil that accompanies them. Our approach has been twofold. First, we offer concrete advice, clearly explaining medical information, care options, and practical decisions that must be made. Of equal importance, however, we stress the opportunities for hope, personal control, and loving family connection that still exist. This book has been written with this same twofold approach in mind.

The first half of the book (chapters 1 through 6) contains information to help you and your loved one better understand crucial medical issues. First, we'll discuss how to navigate a complex and often confusing medical system. We'll introduce you to the various professionals who may be caring for your loved one and help you speak their language. Next, we'll help you to understand your loved one's illness, its symptoms, and potential care options, including choices about where your loved one should live at this time. If you're like many people, you worry about what it will be like as your loved one encounters the final days of life. For this reason, we've also included a chapter on what seriously ill people typically experience as death nears.

The second half of the book (chapters 7 through 12) addresses the many nonmedical but still important issues that you and your loved one may face. Although most of us are taught to "be strong" at times like these, this isn't always easy. What's the normal way to feel when a loved one is dying? Is it okay to share these feelings with your loved one? What should and shouldn't you be saying to him or her? What can you do to renew yourself when you're feeling burnt-out? How can you deal with your grief? Is there any meaning in what's happening? These are just some of the emotional and spiritual questions we'll address. In the midst of this emotional storm, various practical matters also must be addressed, including advance directives, wills, and funeral arrangements. We'll discuss how to manage these tasks as easily as possible, without losing out on important time with your loved one.

Before you read further, we recommend that you purchase a standard-size notebook (8.5 by 11 inches). This will be useful in a couple of ways. First, you may want to jot down important pieces of information as you read. These notes may be helpful as your speak with your loved one and his or her health care providers. Second, many chapters contain exercises designed to help you consider important medical, practical, and emotional issues. When you come to these exercises, you'll want to have a place to record your thoughts.

In writing this book, we've tried to keep in mind the many complex and emotional situations that our readers may be facing. Each chapter begins with a brief story—a composite of our shared encounters—about a family confronting an important issue. The remainder of the chapter then addresses this issue with information and specific guidance. Some people may wonder whether it's best to read the book all the way through or skip to particular chapters of interest. Although reading the book cover to cover will give you the most complete information, use the book in whatever way feels right. If there's a pressing issue, feel free to skip to the chapter that covers it. Most of the chapter titles speak for themselves. No matter how you use the book, we sincerely hope that our words provide valuable information, guidance, and comfort as you walk alongside your loved one on a difficult but potentially very meaningful journey.

CHAPTER 1

Could the Doctors Be Wrong?

Understanding and Coming to Terms with Bad News

Charlie had done everything right. He worked hard in school, excelled in college, and built his own accounting business from the ground up. He and his wife Evelyn had raised two fine boys, both Eagle Scouts. Kevin, his oldest, had just started his first year of college, and Bryan was entering his sophomore year of high school. Both played basketball and actively volunteered at church. With his sons' encouragement, Charlie had become a vegetarian. He worked out routinely and even had lost twenty-five pounds two years ago, and more weight recently. At forty-six years old, everything seemed to be going well. Except now his doctor was sitting in front of him, speaking earnestly and from her heart: Charlie had cancer, and it didn't look good at all.

"We've received the results back from Monday's biopsy," said Dr. Horta. "It confirmed a poorly differentiated adenocarcinoma. We're not sure where in the body it came from, but we'll need to start chemotherapy right away."

Charlie wasn't prepared to hear anything like this. Barely a week ago, he'd been obsessing over changes in the tax code. He'd assumed his ulcer was acting up again, causing the discomfort that sent him to the doctor. What was an adenocarcinoma? What about it was "poor"? And what did "differentiated" mean? He was thankful that his wife, Evelyn, was with him so she could ask these questions.

"Can chemotherapy get rid of it?" she asked.

"It's pretty severe. Although I'm hopeful we can force things into remission, I think you need to prepare for the worst," said Dr. Horta. "I'm planning on admitting you to the hospital this afternoon, and we may even start chemotherapy tonight. We may also need to get another scan done."

"Has the cancer spread anywhere else?" asked Evelyn. "Is that what you're looking for?"

Dr. Horta paused and took a deep breath before she spoke. "The first scan showed a spot in the liver and another on one of Charlie's adrenal glands. But we didn't focus on those areas specifically, so I'm not sure what they are. Also, the back pain Charlie's been having may be from the tumor itself, so we'll want to do a bone scan to make sure it hasn't spread to the spine."

Evelyn stifled a cry and swallowed. Charlie had lost himself in discouraging thoughts. "What if it has spread to my liver? What if there's cancer in my spine? Is this something that could . . ." The questions in his mind trailed off.

"I'm going to beat this thing," said Charlie, emerging from a daze. "I'm going to beat this. Whenever we've had problems, we've gotten through them on faith. I believe in God and I am going to beat this thing."

Dr. Horta nodded her head, but her gaze didn't match her gesture. "It's great to be thinking that way. It's going to be a tough few weeks, and positive thinking will help. Once we get you admitted, our infusion nurse will discuss the specifics of chemotherapy and get your consent. Charlie, why don't you start on the paperwork now?"

Charlie got up slowly and ambled toward the front desk. Evelyn couldn't believe how sick he looked. How had she missed it? When Charlie lost ten pounds, she just figured he was exercising more and staying away from donuts. As Charlie left the room, Evelyn and Dr. Horta stayed seated.

"Dr. Horta," said Evelyn, "I know things look bad. But Charlie and I have faith and we both believe in miracles. Just do everything you can."

HOPING FOR MIRACLES

In our darkest moments, we all fear being in Charlie's situation: sitting in front of a doctor and hearing the crushing details of a life-threatening illness. As we age, we hear more of these horrible stories—the wife of a colleague from work, a former college roommate, a close friend's father. Sometimes members of our own families are the ones sitting in front of doctors, lying in hospital beds, awaiting biopsy results, receiving bad news, and hoping for miracles. Because you're reading this book, it's likely that you also bear the burden of bad news and may be hoping the doctors are mistaken about your loved one's future.

We read about miracles all the time. People return from the brink of death, reporting a bright white light or a welcoming relative. Patients whom physicians have declared terminally ill sometimes recover to outlive the grimmest prognoses. These stories inspire patients and families to maintain hope, and they motivate health care professionals to work even harder. We all recognize, however, that we are mortal and that modern medicine, miraculous though it seems, has limits. We also know that because of medicine's advances, fewer of us will die suddenly from a heart attack or stroke than in past decades. More of us—our parents, our siblings, our friends, ourselves—will, like Charlie and his wife, be forced to interpret bad news about a slowly progressing condition.

Patients and families have a wide range of normal reactions to hearing bad news. Some want to know as much as possible about the future. Others may prefer to remain in the present, deferring or avoiding any discussion about prognosis. Good physicians respect people's feelings, inquiring about what information they desire to know and at what pace. Most doctors recognize a certain amount of ambivalence in these patients: the need for hope paired with the desire to understand their disease and its timing. As you and your loved one face this situation, we recommend adopting the attitude "hope for the best and plan for everything." This book is dedicated to providing information and advice for doing just that.

GETTING ALL THE INFORMATION

When informed of a loved one's serious illness, you may wish to find out more information from the doctor. Unfortunately, doctors don't always communicate with patients and families as effectively as possible (and vice versa). This can occur for lots of reasons. Sometimes the fault lies with doctors: They may use overly technical jargon or fail to spend sufficient time answering questions. On the other hand, sometimes patients and family members can't think of the right questions to ask, or they may feel so intimidated by the whole process that they remain quiet. If you've experienced any of these situations, you know how frustrating they can be. Nonetheless, it's usually worth making another effort to communicate effectively with your loved one's physician. In the next chapter, we'll offer detailed advice about how to maximize your time with the doctor. For now, we'd like to offer some pointers to help you through the first few conversations:

- Be on time. If the appointment feels rushed, consider politely asking for more time or a second appointment.

- Be assertive, rather than angry or threatening. Remember that physicians are people too, fraught with the same insecurities and emotions as everyone else. Though it's trite, it's also true: You can usually catch more bees with honey than with vinegar.

■ Ask the physician to summarize the medical situation prior to beginning a dialogue. This will help clarify any misunderstandings or disagreements before decision making begins.

■ If you don't understand the terms a physician uses, politely request clarification. Ask for information in layman's terms rather than medical jargon.

■ If you feel you aren't getting a straightforward answer, this may be more a reflection of the doctor's own uncertainty rather than any disregard for you. To put the doctor at ease, use statements like "It's okay if you're not sure" or "I'm sure it's hard to say, but . . ." Then continue to ask for as precise an answer as possible.

■ Finally, feel free to sleep on it. Although some medical decisions must be made right away, most can be held off for a few days while you take time to process your feelings. Waiting may enable you to ask better questions, carefully consider the important information you receive, and ultimately make better decisions.

You and your loved one deserve meaningful, effective communication with physicians. Your questions should be answered thoroughly and compassionately, and your hopes, fears and anxieties should be addressed. Although it's important to respect the doctor's perspective, meaningful dialogue is a right, not a gift. If you're not getting answers to your questions, consider politely making this clear.

UNDERSTANDING THE PROGNOSIS

If you wish to know more about your loved one's prognosis, the best strategy is to directly ask the physician. With this said, it's important to realize that doctors aren't very good at predicting how long someone will live.

They're only human and can only make an educated guess. For this reason, they may be reluctant to answer directly, saying things like "It's hard to say" or "It's in God's hands." Most patients and families wish for something more concrete. Nonetheless, the doctor is probably being honest. Noted end-of-life care specialist Dr. James Hallenbeck (2003) likens physicians to weathermen, and it's easy to understand the comparison. Given specific data—diagnosis, age, general health, and so on—doctors may be able to tell you the average life expectancy for someone in your loved one's situation. What will actually happen in your loved one's particular case, however, is anybody's guess. The doctor may not know the specific nature of your loved one's disease, the complications it may cause, or the emotional strengths and spiritual reserves he or she may bring to the situation.

As the storm front nears, doctors may gain greater insight regarding the future. Good physicians use all the available information combined with their own experience to provide a range of possible times. They may estimate "months to years" or "hours to days." Boldly asserting narrower windows can mislead patients and families, causing mistrust of the physician and misuse of time. Keep this in mind when inquiring about prognosis, and you'll have an easier time riding the waves of uncertainty.

Words Describing Prognosis

When discussing your loved one's condition, the doctor may use a variety of unfamiliar terms. Given the emotional nature of the situation, it's easy to get lost in the jumble of words, emerging from medical conversations with precious little understanding. Throughout this book, we'll offer sections dedicated to giving you the vocabulary you'll need. Let's begin with some basic terms describing illnesses and their prognoses.

CHRONIC ILLNESS

Chronic illness refers to any disease that a patient lives with over an extended period of time, managing daily complications and symptoms with the help of health care providers. Chronic illnesses include some cancers, heart failure, emphysema, arthritis, diabetes, and dementia, among others.

When doctors refer to a disease as chronic, the unstated assumption is that it probably can't be cured. Rather, efforts are directed at managing the disease, preventing flare-ups, reducing the need for hospitalization, and maximizing functioning and quality of life for the patient.

ACUTE ILLNESS

In contrast to chronic diseases, acute illnesses may be curable or short-term. Many acute illnesses, such as pneumonia, urinary tract infections, and appendicitis, result from infections. Sudden heart attacks or strokes leading to complications that subside somewhat also may fall into this category. Acute illnesses frequently occur among people who have an ongoing chronic disease. People suffering from diabetes, for example, have a higher incidence of heart attacks and infections. Likewise, patients with lung cancer may develop pneumonia.

When acute illnesses occur against a backdrop of chronic illness, it can be very hard for families and even doctors to know what to do. If a woman with no significant health problems develops severe pneumonia, it probably makes sense to subject her to the sometimes uncomfortable and distressing intensive care procedures necessary to treat this disease. She may be placed on a breathing machine, receive multiple antibiotics, have blood drawn frequently, have large IVs inserted into her neck or chest, and have fluid drained from around her lungs. Nonetheless, it will almost certainly be worth it, allowing her to recover and live for many years with a high quality of life.

On the other hand, if that same woman has advanced lung cancer that has spread to her bones and liver, has lost forty pounds in the last three months, and will probably not be able to get out of bed again, the picture is much more complicated. The procedures necessary to treat her pneumonia will most likely not improve her cancer or her quality of life. Nevertheless, these procedures could still make sense. She could be hoping to stay alive for the birth of a grandchild or for her eighty-fifth birthday. But more probably, such procedures would only prolong physical suffering. In later chapters, we'll offer guidance for families facing difficult decisions like this one.

TERMINAL ILLNESS

If you're like most people, "terminal" may be the scariest word imaginable. Nonetheless, the term isn't clear-cut and may not mean exactly what you think. For instance, many chronic illnesses technically can be thought of as terminal, meaning that they can't be fully eradicated from the body and are likely to be the ultimate cause of death. Nonetheless, physicians rarely use this term unless they believe a patient is in the final few months of life.

Some cancers are considered terminal when they're first diagnosed because they aren't curable with current technology. Although about twenty percent of patients with newly diagnosed stage III lung cancer will survive for five years or more, this disease is technically terminal. Other diseases, like heart failure and dementia, may have survival rates similar to many cancers, yet they are rarely thought of as terminal. At the time of diagnosis, most doctors consider these diseases chronic and manageable even though long-term survival often mirrors that of "terminal" cancer. Most physicians consider the goal of treatment for many chronic illnesses to be preventing their progression, keeping them from entering the terminal stage. Because of the inherently confusing nature of the word "terminal," don't hesitate to ask what a doctor means when using it.

SECOND OPINIONS

Upon hearing bad news, it's natural to wonder if the doctor could be wrong or overly pessimistic. Would other doctors concur with the diagnosis? Would they agree with the recommended treatment? Are there other options available that the first doctor isn't telling you about? These are just a few of the many questions that might flash through your mind.

Many people fear that asking for a second opinion will offend the primary physician. In our experience, however, most doctors are happy to accommodate this request, especially when it concerns serious and complex medical issues. A little-known fact is that physicians seek out the opinions of colleagues all the time without you realizing it. Even if the doctor does take offense, that shouldn't interfere with requesting a second opinion if you feel you'd like one. A serious diagnosis has far-reaching ramifications for patients and their families, and your confidence in the diagnosis is ultimately more important than protecting the doctor's feelings. If you don't have a specific doctor in mind, it's a good idea to ask for someone outside of the first doctor's practice group or clinic. Sometimes there are insurance hurdles to surmount, although most plans provide coverage for second opinions.

If you would like to pursue a second opinion, the first step is to carefully consider *why* this is important to you. There are a number of reasons why you might wish to seek out another expert's input:

- The diagnosis is unclear or there are no clear treatment options.

- The diagnosis is uncommon and may require a particular expert's opinion.

- Communication with the first physician is uncomfortable or ineffective.

- A second opinion would allow you and your loved one to feel more confident about the diagnosis or the treatment options being offered.

- The input of another physician would allow you and your loved one to more confidently choose among the treatment options.

When asked to provide a second opinion, some doctors prefer to approach the case blindly, not knowing the first doctor's diagnosis or treatment plan. Others prefer to have this information at hand. In any case, be prepared to provide medical records, X-rays, and any other information requested by the second physician. This usually entails signing documents to have the information sent from one health care provider to another, though occasionally you may need to hand carry these materials.

After seeking out a second opinion, you may or may not find that the doctors agree. Be careful not to "doctor shop" or solicit only those opinions you agree with. If the opinions differ, before leaping to the second doctor for care, ask the first doctor why there is a difference of opinion. The second doctor may not have all of the available information or may be making decisions in a vacuum, without the benefit of the first doctor's history with your loved one. It's never easy to hear negative information, but that doesn't mean it's incorrect.

MAKING DECISIONS FOR YOUR LOVED ONE

If you've picked up this book, you're probably facing the possibility of caring for or making decisions for your loved one. For a variety of reasons, people who are very sick sometimes can't make big decisions by themselves. Your loved one may suffer from chronic dementia. Or, because of a combination of illness, medications, and other factors, your loved one may not be able to consider matters as he or she once could. Even when they're capable, some people prefer that their relatives make medical decisions for them or help with the process. Analyzing medical information can be tiring, dispiriting, or just plain confusing even when you're well.

If you've agreed to make medical decisions for your loved one or help with making them, we want to acknowledge your caring and your courage. The job isn't easy, but it's often a necessary one. It will be important to remember that your job isn't to make decisions according to your own values or personal philosophy, but to serve the needs and desires of your loved one as best you understand them. Although you may experience a roller coaster of emotions when facing difficult choices, keeping this basic principle in mind may provide some clarity. Whether you're making decisions, helping your loved one make decisions, or just providing support, it will be useful for you to understand the roles of various medical professionals—the topic of the next chapter.

CHAPTER 2

Who Are All These People?

Making Sense of the Medical System and Its Many Faces

When Sara arrived at the hospice facility, her daughter helped her get settled into her new room. Sara had severe emphysema, a lung condition that had slowly worsened over the years. As she started to weaken, it became obvious that her daughter and son-in-law could no longer manage her care. Because Sara knew that she would probably pass away within a few months, she chose to enter an inpatient hospice close to home. Although she felt good about this decision, actually being admitted was a big step—one that made Sara very anxious.

She was most anxious about her medications. When she learned that she would have a new doctor in hospice, she became frightened that he might take away her "miracle pills." Because of the emphysema, Sara had trouble breathing. Although the tube perched beneath her nose helped bring the oxygen in her blood to normal levels, she still felt short of breath. When she couldn't catch her breath, she felt terrified and would tense up, making it seem even harder to breath. Several months ago, her general practitioner had prescribed a tranquilizer, which helped her relax and eased her hunger for air.

Even after her daughter left for the day, Sara continued to clutch a small paper bag filled with these pills. She asked the first person in a white coat who entered the room if it was okay to continue taking them. Relieved to hear that the answer was yes, she placed the paper bag on the table beside her bed and, before long, drifted off to sleep.

Three hours later, Sara awoke to see a nurse standing over her. "I'm sorry to wake you, but I have some medicine for you to take," the nurse said kindly.

Sara stretched a little, took the pills from the nurse, and swallowed them. "I think I took a little nap. What time is it?" Sara asked.

"It's about 5:30. Your dinner should be coming soon."

Because she usually took her tranquilizer before dinner, Sara pointed to the small bag on her nightstand. "Would you mind handing that to me? I usually take one of those too," Sara said.

"One of what?" the nurse inquired, looking slightly alarmed.

"A pill for my nerves."

"Oh, sorry. I don't think your chart has an order for that. I'll have to ask your doctor about it. Let me take these for now, and maybe we can give you one later tonight or tomorrow."

"But I already asked the doctor, and he said it was okay if I took them," Sara said, worried and a little annoyed.

"Which doctor did you ask?"

Sara searched her memory. She couldn't recall the doctor's name, so she described him.

The nurse thought for a moment. "Oh, he's not your doctor. He's just the resident who's rotating through the unit this month. He doesn't really know how we do things yet. I promise I'll check with the doctor as soon as I can, and we'll start the medication if he says it's all right. Okay?"

Sara reluctantly agreed, feeling more anxious than she had in a long time. And as the nurse left, Sara thought, "What is a resident, anyway?"

DISPELLING SOME OF THE CONFUSION

In today's medical system, experiences like Sara's are common. Who should you speak to if there's a problem? The nurse? The doctor? Is a resident the same as a doctor? Who exactly has the power to get things done? All too often, health care agencies seem confusing and impersonal even though they're composed of professionals who genuinely want to help.

In this chapter, we hope to make the medical system a little less confusing. First we'll discuss the many types of health care professionals you'll encounter. Next, we'll offer practical tips for how to talk to these professionals, especially your loved one's doctor. And finally, we'll discuss how to include the whole family in the medical conversation.

THE HEALTH CARE TEAM: KNOW WHO YOU'RE TALKING TO

Doctors, nurses, social workers, specialists in rehabilitation, psychotherapists, and chaplains all may be involved in your loved one's care. These professionals form a team that meets regularly to share information and plan treatment. Although most people agree that more care is better than less, the sheer number of individuals potentially caring for your loved one can seem overwhelming. Knowing more about each of their roles may make the situation more manageable.

Doctors

The doctor is the final authority on your loved one's care. Everyone knows what a doctor is, right? If you're like most people, you've seen a doctor at least once a year since childhood. Nonetheless, you may find yourself confused when one doctor says she's an attending physician, another says he's a resident, and yet another claims she's a specialist. Which one, exactly, is the "real" doctor? Read on for help answering this question.

ATTENDING PHYSICIANS

Attending physicians, also simply called attendings, are what most of us think of as a doctor. These fully licensed medical professionals care for patients in a variety of settings, including clinics, hospitals, nursing homes, and hospices. In facilities affiliated with universities or other academic institutions, attending physicians also supervise doctors in training. Your loved one's primary doctor will almost always be an attending physician. Even if most of the care is performed by nurses or residents, the attending physician ultimately is responsible for this care.

RESIDENT PHYSICIANS

A resident physician, also known simply as a resident, has graduated from medical school and has received a doctoral degree but is still in training. Although medical school gives doctors immense knowledge, basic clinical skills, and some experience practicing medicine, an additional three or more years of residency is necessary to complete their education. The first year of residency is often called an internship, so you also may hear some residents described as interns.

In some situations, the doctor most directly responsible for the care of your loved one may be a resident. Is a resident a real doctor? Yes, very much so. You can feel very comfortable trusting most residents' judgment, especially because they're closely supervised by attending physicians. Unfortunately, because residents rotate through various departments of a health care facility, a particular resident may be assigned to your loved one for only a month or two. Generally, this isn't a problem because many of the providers on the health care team, including the attending physician in most cases, will continue working with your loved one throughout his or her care. Nonetheless, you may have to explain your loved one's medical situation to a new resident every few weeks. If you're uncomfortable with this, feel free to speak with the attending physician. It may be possible for the team to provide more continuity in your loved one's care.

MEDICAL STUDENTS

In order to become doctors, medical students must complete at least four years of school beyond college. Medical students typically begin seeing patients on a limited basis during their first year of medical school; their responsibilities increase dramatically in the final two years. Although a medical student will never be your loved one's primary doctor, he or she may perform certain medical procedures or observe a doctor providing care. Although you generally can feel confident about the expertise of medical students, if you don't want a student to be more than minimally involved in your loved one's care, feel free to request this.

SPECIALISTS

Some doctors focus on patients' medical care as a whole, whereas others concentrate on a specific disease or type of treatment. Although there are differences between them, primary care doctors, family physicians, internists, and hospitalists are all concerned with patients' care as a whole. Similarly, geriatricians are physicians who have special training in managing the overall care of elderly patients. Although these professionals frequently have training in specific areas beyond those necessary to be a general medical doctor, you can think of them as general doctors because they routinely treat a wide array of medical problems. Specialists, on the other hand, are experts in specific aspects of medicine. For instance, oncologists specialize in cancer, cardiologists focus on heart conditions, and nephrologists are experts in kidney problems. Depending on your loved one's needs, his or her primary doctor may or may not be a specialist. Either way, your loved one's physician may choose to consult additional specialists if expertise in a particular area is needed.

PHYSICIAN ASSISTANTS, NURSE PRACTITIONERS, AND CLINICAL NURSE SPECIALISTS

Although physician assistants, nurse practitioners, and clinical nurse specialists aren't doctors, they're licensed to perform many of the same duties. Depending on the state in which they practice, they may diagnose diseases, prescribe medications, and even perform minor surgery. They typically work closely with doctors, and sometimes they're required to be supervised by doctors. In some medical settings, such as clinics and emergency rooms, it's typical for physician assistants or nurse practitioners to serve in the role of primary doctor, even though they're not physicians. Don't be alarmed if you encounter this situation. These professionals are usually well trained and credentialed, and they may have considerable experience.

Nurses

Nurses come in three basic varieties. Registered nurses (RNs) have the most education. They perform tasks ranging from bathing and changing patients to giving shots and inserting IV lines. Historically, RNs have played a prominent role in hospice care, and they frequently serve as chief administrators of hospice agencies. Licensed practical nurses (LPNs), sometimes also called licensed vocational nurses (LVNs), have somewhat less education and tend to perform less medically complex tasks than RNs. Finally, certified nursing assistants (CNAs), who have the least training, primarily address the practical needs of patients. They aren't licensed to perform medical procedures involving medicine or needles, for example.

Social Workers

Social workers provide a wide range of nonmedical services to help patients and their families balance the complexities of medical care with the practicalities of everyday life. Their assistance can be useful in thinking through general goals of care, considering where your loved one will live, drafting advance directives, or making a last will and testament. Some social workers also provide psychotherapy. If you have a question about your loved one's care that doesn't directly involve medical issues, a social worker is probably the right person to talk to. Social workers are among the best-connected health care professionals, so even if they can't answer a question, they'll probably know who can.

Physical Therapists, Occupational Therapists, and Speech Therapists

Physical therapists, occupational therapists, and speech therapists are experts in rehabilitation. If a patient loses the ability to walk, speak clearly, bathe independently, or function in other important ways, one of these therapists might be consulted. By guiding patients through special exercises, offering practical advice, and providing guidance on the purchase and use of special adaptive equipment, these therapists can help people be as independent as possible.

Psychotherapists

Psychotherapists specialize in mental health counseling. Several types of professionals call themselves psychotherapists, including psychologists, marriage and family therapists, licensed counselors, and clinical social workers. Psychiatrists are medical doctors who also sometimes provide counseling, though they most frequently care for patients when psychiatric medications are necessary. Depending on their area of specialty, these professionals can provide expert care to both patients and family members for a variety of emotional issues.

Chaplains

Chaplains address the religious and spiritual needs of patients. Typically, they're ordained ministers, priests, or rabbis who have chosen to work in health care. If you or your loved would like to discuss spiritual matters, feel free to request a chaplain of your faith. Unfortunately, no health care agency can employ chaplains of every religion; however, no matter what religion a chaplain is affiliated with, he or she should be comfortable speaking with patients and family members of any faith.

GETTING THE ANSWERS AND SUPPORT YOU NEED

With the large number of providers potentially caring for your loved one, you may wonder whom to approach for help or information. As a general rule, speaking with your loved one's nurse is a good first step. Part of the nurse's job is listening to patients' concerns and relaying them to the proper person on the health care team. If the nurse isn't able to address your concern, ask to talk with your loved one's primary doctor. Because this doctor is in charge of your loved one's care, most major medical decisions eventually will have to be discussed with him or her.

Of course, talking with a doctor can be difficult. Family members sometimes feel intimidated or confused by their loved one's physician. Although many doctors are excellent communicators, others use overly technical language, don't provide complete information, or hurry through complex and confusing details. In the next few pages, we'll provide some tips for communicating effectively with your loved one's physician.

Tip #1: Do Your Homework

Thirty years ago it was commonplace for patients and family members to blindly follow doctors' orders. Because there were fewer medical options, doctors often knew all of them. Increasingly, this situation is changing and one result is that, for better or worse, patients have more authority to direct their own care than ever before—and perhaps more to gain by doing so. But this requires homework.

Consider reading up on your loved one's condition. Chapter 3 of this book should be a good start. Other books, websites, and pamphlets also can be great sources of information. Additionally, if you know people who have faced serious illness before, ask them about their experiences. All of this information will help you decide what questions to ask the doctor.

Tip #2: Have an Agenda

Doctors are extraordinarily busy people, and it's important to use their time wisely. Because most doctors will only be able to talk for about fifteen to twenty minutes at a time, you should prioritize what is most important to discuss. This enables you and the physician to maximize your time together. Of course, while most people have a good idea of what they want to talk about with the doctor, it's easy to forget questions or issues once the doctor is in the room. That's why it's important to write down an agenda. Although this takes preparation on your part, it's well worth the effort. Use the following exercise to help you prepare an agenda.

EXERCISE
Preparing to Speak with a Doctor

The best kind of agenda is a simple list. The advantage of a list is that you can hand it to the doctor so that he or she can be sure to address all of the issues. In fact, research by physician Thomas Wells and colleagues (2004) has shown that doctors also get a lot out of such lists. By having your agenda on paper, doctors can quickly see not only what you want to know, but also what you aren't asking but may need to know.

To make an agenda, open your notebook to a clean page and write "Important Issues" at the top. On the rest of the page, list three to five topics or questions that you would like to cover during your meeting. If you select more than five, you probably won't have time for all of them, so try to choose only the most important ones. Use your best judgment to determine how many items should appear on your agenda. If necessary, write brief notes below each agenda item to remind yourself of any important details that should be discussed. At the beginning of your meeting, be sure to ask the doctor to peruse this list.

Agenda items will vary widely depending on the person, their illness, and other details, but certain issues come up often. Here are a few lists of suggested agenda items:

About the Problem

- What is wrong with my loved one? What is the diagnosis?

- What is causing this problem?

- What are the reasons why you think this is the problem?

- Are there any other explanations besides this diagnosis?

- Should any more tests be performed?

- My loved one is having pain.

- My loved one is having some new problems.

- I think my loved one's condition is getting worse.

About the Options

- What options does my loved one have?

- What are the benefits and risks of each option?

- Which type of treatment is most common for my loved one's problem?

- In your opinion, which options are the best?

- Where is the best place for my loved one to receive care?

- Will my loved one be able to come home?

- What medications is my loved one taking? What do these medications do?

- What side effects of the medications should we watch for?

- Are any of my loved one's symptoms caused by these side effects?

- Will my loved one ever be able to stop taking any of the medications?

- I think the best option for my loved one is . . .

About the Prognosis

- What is likely to happen to my loved one in the future?

- Could the illness get better? Why or why not? If so, how quickly?

- How quickly do you expect the illness to get worse?

- Do you have any general estimate of how long my loved one will live?

- Should we seek a second opinion?

Tip #3: Set an Appointment

If your loved one is living at home, you're probably used to making doctor's appointments. In inpatient facilities, however, doctors may seem to show up with very little warning and even less time to talk. But there is a method to the madness. Try asking a nurse when the doctor normally makes rounds so that you can be in the room to meet with him or her. If you need more time than the doctor can afford during rounds, consider asking for a return visit at a more convenient time. Family members are most often successful when they say something like "Would it be possible to set up a time to meet with you? I have a few questions that I've written down. I think it will take about fifteen minutes." If necessary, you can also arrange an appointment through the physician's secretary or nurse.

Tip #4: Bring Someone with You

Doctors can be intimidating. Because they often seem very sure of their opinions, you may feel pressured to act like you agree even when you don't. If this is the case, consider asking a trusted friend or family member to accompany you to the appointment. Although it isn't absolutely necessary, having someone by your side has major advantages. Your companion can provide moral support, so you'll be more likely to assert yourself when necessary. Your companion also may think of questions or concerns that you've overlooked. And afterward, your companion will be in a great position to help you think through the information you learned from the doctor.

Tip #5: Take Notes

We always encourage patients and their family members to take notes when meeting with doctors. Fifteen minutes pass quickly. Unfortunately, research shows that people generally understand and remember only part of what their doctors say (Lerner et al. 2000). Your notes will remind you of what was discussed and help you make informed decisions. Another option is to tape-record your meeting. This option is significantly less desirable, however, because doctors may be less likely to speak frankly with a tape rolling.

Many Doctors, No Answers

Even if you have an excellent relationship with your loved one's primary doctor, more than one additional doctor may be involved in the care. These doctors are usually specialists who are consulted when expertise in a particular area is needed. Unfortunately, doctors don't always agree. For example, when Rose, who suffered from advanced Alzheimer's disease, fell and broke her hip, two doctors gave her son Tim vastly different opinions. Although Rose had been growing weaker and would probably die in the near future, nobody knew exactly when. While Rose's primary doctor believed the right option was to transfer Rose to an inpatient hospice facility, the surgeon who examined her in the emergency room insisted that hip surgery was urgently necessary and that Rose should remain in the hospital.

Tim was understandably confused and overwhelmed. Luckily, he had some help. He contacted an old friend who was a medical student, described the doctors' differing opinions, and asked for advice. "They're both right, medically speaking," his friend said. "But this isn't a medical decision, it's a values decision."

When it comes to values, doctors can't tell you what choice to make. In fact, there's often no right or wrong decision. Because Tim knew that his mother was going to pass away soon, he needed to consider how she would most want to spend her final days. Would she want to keep fighting, undergoing a potentially painful surgery to live as long as possible? Or would she want to let nature take its course, avoiding the surgery and being as comfortable as possible during whatever time she had left? As soon as Tim realized that this was a values decision and not only a medical one, he knew exactly what his mother would want. Rose hated hospitals and believed strongly in letting God decide when death would come. Tim decided against the surgery and asked Rose's primary doctor to transfer her to hospice, where she received medication to treat her pain and peacefully spent the last few days of her life.

When doctors disagree, it's sometimes because the decision is about values, not simply about medical facts. If you suspect that this is occurring, consider asking the doctors about it directly. They can often tell you if this is the case.

THE OTHER MEMBERS OF THE HEALTH CARE TEAM

So far, we've discussed the official members of the health care team. But we should mention some important unofficial members: you, your loved one, and your family. After all, you are the people most influenced by medical decisions. Of course, it's not always clear how best to get involved. In the remainder of this chapter, we'll discuss one useful way—the family meeting.

The Family Meeting

Family meetings are often a good way of keeping family members informed about your loved one's medical issues and care options. In fact, some physicians regularly recommend and attend such meetings. However, a physician isn't necessary for a productive meeting, and you can certainly hold family meetings on your own.

Although family meetings can be helpful at any time, they're most useful when difficult decisions must be made. Family meetings often are held when a patient is first diagnosed, when the patient is about to be discharged, or when the patient's medical condition changes substantially. If your loved one's doctor has called a family meeting, he or she will probably have an agenda in mind. If you decide to call a family meeting without the doctor, we suggest using the five-step process detailed below. If your loved one is capable of participating, you should include him or her in every step of the process.

STEP 1: PREPARING

Before the meeting begins, there are several issues to address. First, you should decide what the purpose of the meeting will be. Do you wish to share information about the problem? Do you want to tell the family about a treatment already selected? Do you wish to gather opinions about possible care options?

Second, consider who will participate. Generally, it's best to keep the meeting small—six to eight people at a maximum. Although there is no formula for deciding whom to invite, all participants should be people who your ailing loved one would want involved. Call each participant or send an e-mail explaining the purpose of the meeting and suggesting possible meeting times. If you wish to invite your loved one's primary doctor or other health care providers, approach them first to ensure their participation. Also, they may want to organize the meeting themselves.

Once the participants have been selected, you should decide who will lead the meeting. If the physician won't be coming, we suggest choosing someone who is trusted and valued by all parties. Because family meetings typically last only about one to two hours (and less time if the doctor is present), it's important to select a leader who will be able to keep the discussion focused. Additionally, the leader should ensure that the conversation remains respectful and productive.

STEP 2: SETTING THE STAGE

Once everyone has gathered, the leader should convene the meeting, introduce himself or herself, and ask the other participants to do the same. Next, the leader should state the purpose of the meeting. If the purpose is simply to provide information, consider saying something like "We're here to inform you about the medical problems that Anne is experiencing, as well as what treatment she is choosing." Alternatively, if the purpose is to gather participants' opinions about possible care options, try saying something like "We're here to inform you about Anne's health and gather your input about what care options to pursue."

After stating the purpose of the meeting, the leader may wish to set two basic ground rules. First, participants should remain respectful at all times. Because disagreements may arise, it's important to realize that alternative opinions are well-meant and worthy of discussion. Second, participants should be as open as possible. It's essential that people not hold back information or opinions that they feel may be important. They should also feel free to ask questions at any time during the meeting. Before continuing, the leader should take a moment to ensure that all participants agree to the rules and wish to continue the meeting.

STEP 3: DEFINING THE PROBLEM

To ensure that everyone has up-to-date information, the next step is to share the story of the illness. Even when all participants are well-informed, there are almost always facts that some have either misunderstood or forgotten. If in attendance, your sick loved one may wish to tell his or her own story. Otherwise, the leader should be responsible for this. This account should be kept relatively short (about ten minutes) and as factual as possible. Try to communicate all of the important details but, to keep the conversation moving, remain relatively general about less important aspects of the story. After the story has been told, leave a few minutes for participants to ask questions. If participants begin offering their opinions about treatment, the leader can politely ask them to hold those thoughts until all factual questions have been answered. Use the following exercise to help you consider how best to tell your loved one's medical story.

EXERCISE
Telling the Medical Story

If you'll be leading the family meeting, you may wish to write down some notes to help accurately report your loved one's medical situation. Open your notebook to an empty page and write "Medical Facts" at the top. On the rest of the page, list the facts you will need to tell your loved one's medical story. You'll want to include the following pieces of information:

- The name of the illness

- When the illness was diagnosed

- Major symptoms and problems

- Treatments already tried

- What the doctors say is the likely prognosis

Write down whatever information is necessary, but don't go overboard. It's easy to write down so many notes that they're practically unusable during the actual meeting. Because ideally these meetings are open conversations among family members, we usually don't advocate writing out a script. Such rigid wording can hamper the natural flow of conversation. Nonetheless, you may find it useful to write down some words to get your meeting started. Below the medical facts list, consider writing out the first few sentences that you plan to say. Try beginning with something like "In April of last year, Anne began feeling pain in her abdomen. She went to the doctor a couple of weeks later and had some tests . . ."

STEP 4: DISCUSSING OPTIONS

Once all the facts are understood, you can move on to the options at hand. Either the leader or someone appointed by the leader should briefly describe these options, along with their benefits and risks. This discussion can include both medical treatments (medication, surgery, and so on) and nonmedical options, such as where your loved one will live. Because not all participants may know exactly what's meant by terms such as chemotherapy, home care, or hospice, it's important to explain each option briefly in plain language. Participants should be encouraged to ask questions and suggest additional ideas.

Allow participants ample time to make their feelings known. Their values probably will play a large role in this discussion. Someone may assert, for instance, that one care option is right and another is wrong. Because others may have different opinions, disagreements sometimes result. If this occurs, the leader should ask participants to reflect on the *patient's* values. These values, not those of the participants, ultimately should determine what choices are made. If your loved one isn't able to share his or her own opinions, the leader should try saying something like "What would Anne want? What kind of care would be most consistent with her values?"

This portion of the meeting is highly variable in length. If the purpose of the meeting is simply to inform the family of choices that already have been made, you may wish to skip this step altogether. On the other hand, if the purpose is to solicit their help in making these choices, this step may consume most of the meeting.

STEP 5: SUMMARIZING AND CONCLUDING

If left unchecked, some family meetings can last for hours. Because emotionally difficult conversations are exhausting, we recommend that the leader limit the meeting to one to two hours. If additional meetings are needed, a new date can be set. At this point, the leader should briefly summarize the meeting, including what was discussed, any decisions made, and what the next step will be. This is much easier to do if the leader or another participant has taken notes during the meeting. Finally, the leader should end the meeting by sincerely thanking participants for coming.

AN UPHILL BATTLE

Many family members have told us that caring for their loved one feels like an uphill battle. As soon as one problem resolves, another begins. Health care professionals sometimes seem like great allies and other times feel like frustrating impediments. In reality, they're just like you—human beings who are doing their best. Sara, whose story began this chapter, spoke to her doctor the next day and told him about her "miracle pills," and he gladly allowed her to continue taking them. In addition, her daughter asked whom to contact should additional questions arise. By learning a little about the system in the hospice where Sara was being cared for, they were helping Sara's health care providers help them. If you put the information in this chapter to use, you too will be helping providers to give your loved one the care he or she needs, when it's needed.

CHAPTER 3

What Treatments Are Available?

Making Sense of Diseases and Medical Interventions

James was busy at work when he received the first of many phone calls from his mother. "Your father got lost on his way home from the office," she said.

Since that phone call eight years ago, James's father had become progressively more confused and disabled. This once-vibrant, independent man was now living in a nursing home, bed-bound, dependent on his nurses for feeding and personal hygiene. When James's mother had died three years ago, James took his father into his own home. He hired a daytime caregiver and hoped to keep his father under his own roof. But the financial cost was tremendous, and his *own family suffered from the strain. Admitting his father to a nursing home wracked James with guilt.*

That was eighteen months ago. For the first year, his father did surprisingly well. He continued to recognize his son and seemed to take pleasure in visits from his grandchildren. Over the past six months, however, he had sunk deeper into dementia. He spent all day in bed, developed bedsores on his ankles that refused to heal, and had gone into the hospital twice with fevers. After each hospital admission, he returned to the nursing home in worse shape.

Now he had been admitted to the hospital yet again, this time with severe pneumonia. The staff of the nursing home had mentioned that he sometimes choked on his food, and one of his nurses had even suggested a feeding tube. The doctor in the hospital seemed less sure.

"Assuming he gets better from the pneumonia, we could put in a feeding tube," she said. "It's really up to you."

James was confused and upset. He knew his father would prefer to die a natural death rather than be kept alive on a machine, but he had never really considered a feeding tube. His thoughts raced. If his father couldn't eat, would he starve to death? Would he be thirsty if he couldn't swallow? And most of all, why was the doctor leaving it up to him? Wasn't it her job to decide?

WHY IS IT UP TO ME?

A few decades ago, patients placed extreme trust in their physicians, letting them make decisions on their behalf and rarely questioning the outcome. Today, the landscape has shifted. Patients and families play a much greater role in treatment decisions. As a result, you may wind up feeling like James: confused and overwhelmed by this responsibility. You may ask yourself, "What is the *right* decision?" only to discover that there are a multitude of correct answers.

In this chapter, we'll explain a number of life-threatening illnesses along with the most common care options. Depending on the type and severity of your loved one's illness, various options may or may not be appropriate.

The doctor can give you more detailed information about your loved one's special circumstances. If your loved one suffers from one of these conditions, this won't be an easy chapter to read. However, our hope is that by understanding the illness and its potential treatments, you and your loved one will be better able to face whatever the future holds.

CANCER

Depending on the type and location of cancer, physicians specializing in this disease (oncologists) may offer a dizzying number of treatments. It's easy to find this array of options bewildering. If you feel this way, the treatment descriptions offered in the following pages may help provide some clarity.

Surgery for Cancer

Most people have some sort of personal experience with surgery. If your child gets appendicitis or your coworker suffers an inflamed gallbladder, surgeons often can fix the problem for good. Unfortunately, surgery for cancer isn't so simple. Cancers detected early can often be surgically resected (removed). If the surgeon is able to resect the entire tumor, then sometimes the disease is cured. However, the cancer may already have spread from the site where it originated. Doctors use the term metastatic to refer to cancers that have spread to other parts of the body. It can be genuinely crushing when everyone believes a cancer has been cured only to have it return aggressively. For this reason, doctors rarely presume that patients are cured until they survive several years without any cancer regrowth.

Surgery is a less viable option for patients with metastatic cancer. For one thing, it is less likely that all cancerous tissue can be located and removed. In addition, patients with widespread cancer are often too ill to survive major surgery, so doctors usually opt for other treatments. Even after a tumor has spread, however, oncologists may still suggest surgery for a variety of reasons. Sometimes, taking out as much of the cancer as possible will help extend the person's life span. This is true for diseases like ovarian cancer and some colon cancers. Other times, a tumor may have spread to a part of the body where it is causing harmful or uncomfortable symptoms. In this case, though surgery might not prolong life, it could improve quality of life. When surgery (or any other treatment) is intended to treat symptoms but not to cure the illness, physicians refer to it as "palliative." Although palliative surgery may or may not prolong life, it should improve the quality of life.

The decision of whether or not to operate can be difficult. Although surgery is sometimes quite appropriate, other times it would only lead to additional complications or prolonged suffering. If your loved one has lost all of his or her energy or stays in bed most of the day, it's unlikely that surgery will bring back independence and functioning. If you have questions about surgery, it's always appropriate to ask your loved one's doctor. Caring physicians can help you weigh the costs and benefits of surgery.

Chemotherapy for Cancer

Many people have stereotypes of chemotherapy as a barbaric treatment that's worse than the disease. Fortunately, advances in science have led to great improvements in chemotherapy. Briefly, here's how most chemotherapies work: Cancer cells grow more quickly than most of the body's normal cells. Chemotherapy specifically targets cells that multiply rapidly, thus reducing the number of cancer cells.

Diseases such as testicular cancer and lymphoma can frequently be cured with chemotherapy. Although patients with many other cancers can't be cured by chemotherapy alone, they still may be helped by the treatment. Oncologists use the terms response or remission to describe how the cancer reacts to treatment. Typically, partial remission implies that chemotherapy has cut the active cancer to about half of its original size. Complete remission usually means that scans no longer indicate the presence of cancer in the body, though inactive tumors may still remain. Because cancers often come back after complete remissions, oncologists rarely use the word "cured" at this stage. But some responses and remissions last for months or even years; doctors may refer to these remissions as durable.

If your loved one is considering chemotherapy, you're probably concerned about side effects. Chemotherapies often unintentionally destroy healthy cells, leading to hair loss, nausea, or low levels of certain good cells in the blood. Fortunately, doctors can prescribe medicines to help with these side effects. Although there's no way to avoid all side effects, there's also no need for chemotherapy to be as uncomfortable as in the past. It's important to ask the oncologist about each chemotherapy's possible side effects. Encourage the doctor to give specific suggestions for how to deal with them. Nurses may also be able to provide guidance in this regard.

Oncologists usually give chemotherapy in a cycle, so that a certain chemotherapy drug is given to a patient every few weeks. Completing this cycle on schedule offers the best chance for the treatment to work. Nonetheless, the decision to undergo a cycle of chemotherapy is not a signed contract. If your loved one experiences unwanted or unsafe side effects, he or she may choose to stop or delay the treatment. So if you or your loved one are uncertain about the decision, remember that it's okay to stop chemotherapy at any time if the burdens begin to outweigh the benefits.

Moreover, it's important to keep in mind that people with cancer are sometimes too sick to tolerate chemotherapy. The more frail and debilitated patients become, the more likely it is that they will suffer toxic side effects from chemotherapy or become susceptible to infections. If your loved one is experiencing loss of appetite, loss of energy, and significantly low body weight, it may be time to stop aggressive chemotherapy. At the very least, you, your loved one, and the doctor should consider whether chemotherapy is doing more harm than good.

Radiation Therapy for Cancer

Radiation therapy attempts to stop or slow cancer growth by focusing a beam of radiation at tumors. Sometimes, radiation therapy combined with chemotherapy can help cure a cancer. More often, doctors use radiation for palliative purposes. In other words, they hope to improve patients' symptoms, whether or not their life span can be extended. More so than chemotherapy, palliative radiation can provide substantial benefits even later in the progression of the disease. For patients whose cancer has spread to the bones, for instance, radiation can sometimes help with the resulting pain and reduce the need for sedating medications.

Patients don't feel anything when actually undergoing radiation. With newer technology and understanding, side effects from radiation tend to be mild and easily addressed—perhaps some fatigue or nausea, depending on the treatment. Healthier patients can usually manage to go to radiation therapy every day for four to eight weeks. For weaker patients, however, it can be a struggle to visit the radiation center so frequently. Consequently, radiation oncologists sometimes suggest increasing the intensity of the radiation rather than spreading it out over many sessions. It's important to ask your loved one's oncologist about different treatment options, especially if you're worried about the difficulty of a lengthy treatment. As with chemotherapy, if your loved one decides to begin a course of radiation therapy, this does not obligate him or her to complete it. If the burden of transport becomes too great or if your loved one's health declines too much, stopping radiation remains a legitimate option.

With cancer, as with other terminal illnesses, hospice is an option that many people consider at life's end. This form of care, which focuses on maximizing comfort, is discussed later in the chapter.

ORGAN FAILURE

Organ failure doesn't usually conjure the same kind of fear as cancer, especially since people can live with some types of organ failure for years. We've heard many patients say, "I've got a touch of heart failure" or "I've been on the dialysis machine for a while." For this reason, patients, families, and physicians sometimes don't recognize when organ failure transitions from a chronic condition to a terminal illness. As a general rule, if your loved one is suffering more and more complications and experiencing repeated hospitalizations, it's time to begin wrestling with serious questions about prognosis and the goals of medical care. In the next few pages, we offer information that may be helpful as you grapple with these difficult issues.

Heart Failure

The heart is a simple yet necessary muscle that pumps needed blood to the body's many organs and tissues. When the heart is damaged—most commonly by heart attacks, high blood pressure, or alcohol abuse—other organs suffer the consequences. For instance, blood can back up into the lungs and cause difficulty breathing. Additionally, a weak heart may diminish blood flow to the kidneys, which can lead to kidney failure. Over the past decade, scientists have discovered new strategies for controlling heart failure. Still, it remains one of the most common reasons for hospitalization and eventual death.

Patients with heart failure often live with the consequences of their disease for years. Initially, they may feel well on an average day but be sensitive to seasonal allergies or become short of breath with exertion. As heart failure worsens, even the best medical care can't prevent patients from feeling winded with only minimal activity. Their overall state of health may be so fragile that anything—even too much salt or a common cold—can send them to the emergency room. In the final stages of heart failure, these emergencies often grow more frequent. If your loved one suffers from heart failure, you may be considering some of the following options.

HEART TRANSPLANT

For patients below age seventy who are otherwise in good health, heart transplantation may be possible. In specialized medical centers throughout the country, surgeons can remove a failing heart and implant a new one. Although the medications required to maintain a new heart are numerous and have many side effects, transplantation can be a miraculous option for appropriate patients. Unfortunately, only a few thousand heart transplants take place each year, primarily because few donor hearts are available. Also, most people with heart failure are past the age where transplantation is a viable option. Their bodies couldn't survive the stress of a major surgery and the complications that could occur afterward. Although continued research makes transplantation a more attractive option each year, the reality remains that this procedure is not appropriate for most patients with heart failure.

ASSIST DEVICES FOR HEART FAILURE

Left ventricular assist devices, or LVADs, represent a growing opportunity for some patients. These battery-powered devices help pump blood out of the heart and into the rest of the body. Because the number of people who need heart transplants far surpasses the number of available hearts, assist devices were first used to keep patients alive long enough to receive a new heart. Over time, doctors have begun experimenting with these devices as a more permanent solution. Nonetheless, there are significant drawbacks. LVADs are often cumbersome, and they can cause serious medical complications, such as strokes and infections. Much like heart transplantation, assist devices are likely to be successful in only a small number of patients.

MEDICAL MANAGEMENT OF HEART FAILURE

The vast majority of heart failure patients opt for medical management. Typically, patients take a variety of medications, monitor their weight, adhere to a low-salt diet, and visit their health care providers frequently to keep their bodies in equilibrium. Even with the best care, however, heart failure can worsen. Catching the flu, not eating the right diet, or a mild heart attack can all lead to hospitalization.

In the hospital, patients with heart failure typically undergo X-rays, blood work, and heart monitoring to determine the cause of the heart failure. If possible, cardiologists will attempt to correct the root cause of the problem. At the same time, they also may try to ease the heart's burden by lowering blood pressure or by using diuretics, medications that remove excess fluid from the body.

If these treatments are not enough, a patient may be admitted to an intensive care unit, where life support medications delivered continuously through an IV line temporarily improve the pumping of a failing heart in the hope that this will help the heart resume beating more regularly on its own. However, because it doesn't always work out that way, people sometimes must choose between trying to go home connected permanently to IV medication or stopping the medication, which could potentially lead to an earlier death.

People with heart failure and their families sometimes feel like they're stuck in a revolving door. After hospitalization, patients may recover for a period of time only to go back into the hospital again in the near future. They may require weeks in a nursing or rehabilitation facility or need to be moved from their homes to a more supervised setting. Loss of independence is often the most frustrating part of advanced heart failure.

If your loved one's quality of life is suffering in this way, you may find yourself wondering whether the treatment is worth it. A major question that often arises in the final stages of heart failure is whether to return to the hospital for treatment. After numerous lengthy hospital stays, this path can become more burdensome than beneficial. Patients often wish to break the cycle and stay home but fear they will suffer horribly from pain or shortness of breath at the end of life. In reality, there are excellent ways to prevent suffering in the final stages of heart failure. However, doctors can't accurately predict when patients are nearing death. Patients suffering from severe exacerbation of heart failure can appear very near death yet sometimes recover substantially. Accepting this uncertainty is essential for developing a medical plan.

You and your loved one should talk about hopes and goals for care *before* an exacerbation, rather than in the heat of the moment. Chapters 8 and 9 contain guidance on how to discuss such difficult issues. This conversation should focus on quality of life. Even when people can't do all the things they once enjoyed, they're often able to maintain tremendous satisfaction in life and self-fulfillment. On the other hand, having little appetite, being unable to walk from the bed to the bathroom without gasping for air, and constantly being transferred back and forth between nursing home and hospital can be upsetting and lead people to question whether continued treatment is worthwhile. While health care professionals currently are not permitted to assist in hastening a patient's death except in Oregon, choosing to maximize comfort and dignity while not actively prolonging life is a legal and ethical alternative in all states. This option, known as hospice care, is discussed later in the chapter.

Chronic Pulmonary Disease

Chronic pulmonary (lung) disease refers to various conditions including emphysema, chronic bronchitis, and pulmonary fibrosis. The primary symptom of pulmonary disease is shortness of breath even during easy activities. Patients with chronic pulmonary disease may remain stable for months and then, with the slightest infection or allergy, require hospitalization. Most significantly, being short of breath makes people frightened and miserable.

Like other serious illnesses, the prognosis for someone with chronic lung disease is uncertain. During exacerbations of lung disease, patients can appear critically ill but then improve substantially seemingly out of the blue. Nonetheless, as the disease progresses, these periods of intense illness occur more frequently and with greater severity. As patients near the end of their lives, they may require inhalers around the clock or need to visit the hospital several times a month.

LUNG TRANSPLANT

Lung transplantation is sometimes, though not often, an option. Very few lung transplants are performed each year, and eligible patients are generally young and suffer from very specific conditions. Long-term survival after lung transplant, though improving, is still poor. Consequently, lung transplantation isn't common for patients with long-standing lung conditions.

MEDICAL MANAGEMENT OF LUNG DISEASE

The vast majority of patients with chronic pulmonary disease choose medical management. Treatment usually includes bronchodilators, inhaled medications that open up the lungs' airways. If your loved one suffers from lung disease, he or she should be sure to eat an appropriate diet, get enough sleep, and see to other personal needs.

It's also extremely important that your loved one receive timely vaccinations for pneumonia and flu, as infections of the airways—either bronchitis or pneumonia—can cause increased breathlessness and may require hospitalization. Physicians typically prescribe medications to treat these infections and decrease inflammation in the airways. During these flare-ups, patients may require additional oxygen by nasal prongs or a face mask. The hope is that whatever is causing the exacerbation will subside and the patient will be able to leave the hospital for as long as possible.

INTENSIVE CARE FOR LUNG DISEASE

In spite of good treatment, sometimes breathing doesn't improve, and patients and their families face difficult choices. In an intensive care unit, physicians can place patients on a ventilator (a mechanical breathing machine). Because the use of a ventilator involves a tube being inserted through the nose or mouth into the windpipe, patients generally must be kept sedated. The hope is that breathing eventually will return to normal and the machine will no longer be necessary. When this doesn't occur, doctors worry that prolonged sedation and irritation of the windpipe may lead to pneumonia and other complications. They may then discuss the option of performing a tracheostomy. This involves a surgeon placing a hole in the patient's throat through which a tube can be inserted, allowing the person to remain connected to a breathing machine without being sedated. After a tracheostomy, some patients are able to stop using the ventilator and return home. Others can leave the hospital with a portable ventilator. Unfortunately, because many families are understandably reluctant to operate complicated medical equipment, many of these patients end up living in nursing facilities.

Although many patients and families choose life-prolonging medical options such as intensive care, less aggressive options are also available for chronic pulmonary disease. As with other serious illnesses, if a doctor indicates that a patient has six months or less to live, hospice care is also a possibility. We'll discuss hospice in greater detail at the end of this chapter.

Liver Disease

Chronic liver failure usually results from the infectious diseases hepatitis B and C or from years of alcohol consumption, although it has many other less common causes. In its later stages, the symptoms of liver failure usually include an elevated risk of bleeding, fluid in the belly (ascites), dangerous abdominal infections (peritonitis), and bouts of confusion (hepatic encephalopathy). Nonetheless, it's very difficult to predict the course of advanced liver failure; even people with severe symptoms often stabilize in the hospital and return home for weeks or months before the next complication occurs.

LIVER TRANSPLANT

Liver transplantation has become quite common. Although far more people need livers than receive them, patients with severe liver disease are often referred to liver transplantation centers for evaluation. In order to be considered for a liver transplant, patients must be free of drugs and alcohol for six months. They also must demonstrate a strong, supportive network of family and friends who can help care for them after the operation. As with other organ transplants, patients must be young and healthy enough to survive the surgery. Once patients are approved for a transplant, the wait can be excruciating, and some don't survive long enough to receive a liver. Fortunately, medical management of liver failure is also an option.

MEDICAL MANAGEMENT OF LIVER DISEASE

Patients awaiting transplant or those not eligible for transplant rely on the care of hepatologists, physicians specializing in liver conditions. These doctors often use medications to help reduce the fluid that accumulates in the abdomen and legs, improving comfort and lowering the risk of infection. Patients also take medications to reduce the risk of gastrointestinal bleeding. Whenever complications occur, patients go to the emergency room for procedures to diagnose and possibly treat the problem. If patients are awaiting a new liver, treating these complications can extend their lives long enough to receive the organ. Although patients not able to receive a liver are likely to experience numerous flare-ups and several hospital stays, they also may have many months of relatively good quality of life.

Even with excellent medical care, patients with liver disease tend to weaken over time, requiring increased support from medical professionals and family members. Quality of life may suffer as a result. For patients with a prognosis of less than six months, hospice care focused on increasing quality rather than quantity of life remains a viable option. Later in the chapter, we discuss this option further.

Kidney Failure

Kidneys serve to filter toxins from the body. People generally are born with two kidneys, but only one is required for normal living. Unfortunately, infections, exacerbations of heart failure, chronic diabetes, and other diseases can sometimes damage both kidneys. When both kidneys fail, toxins can accumulate in the body and fluid may not be adequately eliminated through urination. Patients become sleepy, itchy, and suffer the effects of fluid overload.

KIDNEY TRANSPLANT

Healthier, younger patients may be eligible for kidney transplantation. While kidney transplants are safer and more common than any other organ transplants, demand for kidneys still outpaces supply. For patients unable to receive a new kidney, kidney doctors (nephrologists) may offer dialysis.

DIALYSIS

When the kidneys fail, a dialysis machine can do their work, removing toxins and excess fluid from a patient's blood. Depending on the type and degree of kidney damage, dialysis may be temporary or it may be needed permanently. Patients who need long-term dialysis typically undergo the treatment three times a week as an outpatient. Dialysis is often very effective, keeping patients relatively healthy for years.

Like most treatments, dialysis has drawbacks. Going back and forth to the dialysis center three times a week may become burdensome for some chronically ill people, though having strong social support helps tremendously. Additionally, patients on dialysis can suffer bloodstream infections and sometimes experience dangerously low blood pressure. Medical complications such as these are more common in patients who are already very ill. For a great many patients, however, dialysis is safe and beneficial for both quantity and quality of life.

KIDNEY FAILURE AT THE END OF LIFE

Even with dialysis, kidney failure can still be life threatening. Often, kidney failure is only a small part of a patient's declining health; dialysis may treat the kidney failure but fail to alter the bigger picture. Other times, patients may quite reasonably refuse dialysis in spite of its life-sustaining effects. Perhaps they wish to avoid further surgeries or lengthy trips to a dialysis clinic, or maybe their quality of life is so low that they wish to allow nature to take its course. In general, passing away from kidney failure is peaceful. Patients usually become sleepier and lapse into a coma within a few days or a couple of weeks. Physicians often identify this as their own, wished-for way to die. Many patients who refuse or terminate dialysis enroll in hospice in order to receive in-home care focused on relieving any uncomfortable symptoms. More information on hospice care can be found at the end of the chapter.

DEMENTIA

Watching a loved one succumb to dementia is genuinely heartbreaking. There are very few strains in life more intense than the responsibility of caring for a husband, wife, partner, or parent with advanced dementia. As we will discuss in chapter 7, it's important to expect a wide range of emotions. Know that this roller coaster of feelings is most likely normal and take steps to care for yourself.

Dementia arises from several different diseases, most commonly Alzheimer's disease, vascular dementia (a series of small strokes), and Parkinson's disease. Although neuropsychologists can conduct tests to clarify the particular type of dementia, most dementia is irreversible, so knowing the cause may not be useful in guiding care decisions. Of course, physicians will want to rule out treatable causes of dementia as soon as it's discovered. But given that you're reading this book, most of this workup has probably been completed and you may be dealing with some of the consequences of advanced disease.

Noted palliative care physician David Weissman (2003) uses an alternative term for dementia: brain failure. Like any other organ, the brain performs tasks vital for life. When the brain fails to carry out these responsibilities, various problems arise. Early in the course of dementia, brain failure may cause slight difficulty in remembering names or making accurate judgments. As dementia progresses, people may no longer recognize their family members' faces or they may lose the ability to make reasonable decisions. Ultimately, they may become bed-bound, forgetting how to use their muscles. In the final stages of dementia, brain failure often causes a weak and ineffective swallow, leading to aspiration, wherein food or saliva repeatedly "goes down the wrong pipe." Aspiration can cause pneumonia and shortness of breath. Watching someone struggle in this way can be extraordinarily painful. Knowing what to expect, however, can make the process somewhat easier to cope with.

Here's a typical example: An eighty-five-year-old woman with severe dementia is brought to an emergency room because the staff at her nursing home notices that she's more confused than usual. She's cold and clammy and her blood pressure is very low. By the time her daughter arrives an hour later, the physician appears sad.

"Your mother is very ill," the doctor says. "We've started her on antibiotics, and I'm worried that she may have to go to the intensive care unit if her blood pressure doesn't get better. We may need to put her on a ventilator. I don't know if you and she have ever talked about it, but we need to know how much to do for her. Do you want us to do everything we can?"

This scenario repeats itself in emergency rooms across the country. Unfortunately, "Do you want us to do everything we can?" isn't the right question. A better question might be "What would your loved one want at this point in her life?" If the family believes that she would want to be alive for the imminent birth of her great-grandson, then doing everything to prolong her life makes sense. On the other hand, if she would want to pass away peacefully without repeated hospital admissions, then doing everything to ensure her comfort while avoiding intensive interventions makes more sense. Intensive care, hydration, tube feeding, life support, hospice care—these are merely the means to achieving a goal. What your loved one would want should drive the choices you make.

Intensive Care for Advanced Dementia

Patients with advanced dementia often suffer from recurring infections, most commonly urinary tract infections, aspiration pneumonias, and bone infections resulting from the skin breakdown that can occur when people spend prolonged periods in bed. These infections can be life threatening if they become severe. Sometimes health care providers can treat these infections with antibiotics and intravenous fluids alone. Other times, treatment may require that the patient be admitted to an intensive care unit.

Intensive care units are capable of providing increased nursing care, continuous monitoring of vital signs, as well as ventilator and vasopressor support. Ventilators are machines that take over the responsibility of breathing for a patient who cannot, and vasopressors are medications that elevate a patient's blood pressure to help keep him or her alive. These two interventions are often referred to as life support. Of course, intensive care has drawbacks. It often requires multiple IV lines and a breathing tube inserted through the nose or mouth. Because of the discomfort associated with these measures, patients often are given sedatives or medications for pain control. Unfortunately, these medications can further increase confusion.

Beyond that, patients with these complications don't always improve. Sometimes infections simply overwhelm their weakened bodies. Other times, the physical stress of infection can trigger additional problems, such as heart attacks, heart failure, and kidney failure. These problems can lead to even more intensive care. Again, if you're confronted with difficult medical decisions, it's important to ask yourself, "What would my loved one want?" Of course, asking the doctors and nurses about the likelihood of achieving a particular outcome is equally important. Make sure you know both what you're hoping for and what the medical professionals are expecting; this will help you make sound decisions.

Nutrition and Hydration

Because many patients with advanced dementia have difficulty swallowing and eating, doctors may suggest using a feeding tube. A feeding tube can be placed into the stomach either through the nose or directly through the skin of the abdomen. Ideally, as a patient improves, artificial feeding is no longer needed. Unfortunately, most people with advanced dementia reach a point where they won't recover the ability to swallow effectively. Families often face a brutal choice: Use a feeding tube or accept that their loved one won't be able to eat. This is a very difficult decision, so let's discuss some important details.

First, families often believe that if their ailing loved one doesn't take food or liquid by mouth, there is no longer any risk of breathing it into the lungs and contracting an aspiration pneumonia. Unfortunately, feeding tubes themselves don't prevent aspiration pneumonia. While they do allow liquid food and medicines to pass directly into the stomach, bypassing the mouth, they do nothing to prevent aspiration of saliva. As a healthy person, you probably don't realize that you're constantly swallowing saliva; it's a reflex much like blinking. Patients who can't swallow effectively often have their saliva go down the wrong pipe whether or not they take food by mouth. Accordingly, it isn't surprising that extensive research fails to prove that feeding tubes and artificial nutrition prolong life in the final stages of dementia (Finucane, Christmas, and Travis 1999).

Second, feeding tubes can be uncomfortable. For an already confused person, a feeding tube sometimes can cause more agitation and restlessness. Often, patients will attempt to remove the tube, requiring doctors to use restraints or sedatives to prevent them from doing so. Although this isn't always necessary, witnessing a loved one restrained in this way can be quite upsetting.

Third, doctors remain uncertain whether patients dying of dementia actually experience hunger. Unlike people with end-stage cancer, who almost always say that they no longer care about eating, patients with advanced dementia are unable to tell us if they're hungry. Consequently, it can be extremely difficult for family members to deny their loved one food. Luckily, health care professionals rarely suggest withholding food. While no definitive scientific studies have been performed, we believe that when patients with advanced dementia are carefully fed small amounts of food by hand, they live as long as patients with feeding tubes (DiBartolo 2006). It's often distressing to families that their loved one is not eating a normal amount of food. Even small amounts of food, however, can be sufficient. Nonetheless, your emotional reaction is completely understandable. Whether or not to use a feeding tube is a very difficult matter and requires careful thought.

Hydration and intravenous fluids are just as controversial for these patients, involving both benefits and potential risks. Maintaining an IV often requires that a patient stay in a hospital or nursing home, and sometimes necessitates sedation or use of restraints. Vigorous hydration at the very end of life can also lead to fluid overload as excess water fills the lungs and extremities.

Do IV fluids and tube feeding prolong life at such times, or simply prolong the dying process? The fact that a person can't adequately eat or drink at a late stage of any illness may indicate that the dying process has already begun. For patients with truly end-stage dementia, a feeding tube will rarely enhance quality of life or significantly increase quantity of life. If your loved one's condition is this severe, it's important to consider whether a feeding tube is what he or she would want.

DNR, DNI, AND OTHER LIMITATIONS ON MEDICAL CARE

Patients with a variety of chronic illnesses are sometimes placed on life support in the ICU, such as a ventilator or feeding tube. Ideally, these measures are temporary, with the patient eventually returning to better health. Unfortunately, many patients continue to decline, and families are faced with decisions about withdrawing care. This is a misleading phrase, however. Withdrawing a particular medical intervention should never be equated with withdrawing overall care. If anything, efforts to relieve symptoms should accelerate when other types of treatment are withdrawn. Nonetheless, the decision to withdraw some form of life support can be gut-wrenching for family members, even when it's clear that ongoing intensive care won't bring their loved one back.

Many patients don't wish to set any limits on the length or extent of care. For others, however, setting such limits ahead of time is critical. Some patients may decide that they're willing to go to the emergency room or hospital, but they wouldn't wish to be connected to a breathing machine. Moreover, were their heart to stop beating normally, they might not want cardiopulmonary resuscitation (CPR) or for doctors to attempt to shock their heart back into rhythm. Such requests are generally known as DNR/DNI (do not resuscitate/do not intubate) orders.

If your loved one makes this choice, it's important to have paperwork documenting it. Without such paperwork, paramedics, emergency room personnel, and even hospice nurses must proceed with resuscitation, potentially acting against your loved one's desires. If possible, your loved one should designate one family member or friend to act as a health care proxy. If your loved one is unable to make decisions at any point, this person will be able to communicate his or her wishes to medical providers, including any DNR/DNI orders. Be sure to read chapter 9 for more information on this topic.

If you're like many people, you may worry that DNR/DNI orders are essentially the same as saying, "Do not care for this patient." Nothing could or should be further from the truth. Patients who come to the hospital with such orders still receive all other treatments and life-prolonging measures.

Patients are only placing limits on how to receive care, not denying themselves care! It's also important to note that DNR/DNI orders can be reversed with a verbal request, even when such orders have been signed on paper.

DO NOT REHOSPITALIZE REQUESTS

Hospitals aren't the most pleasant places to spend time. With the lack of privacy, repeated tests, and separation from family, it's easy to understand why some people choose to avoid hospitals altogether. If hospitalization becomes more of a burden than a benefit, patients can request a do not rehospitalize order. As with DNR/DNI orders, such a request doesn't indicate that medical care ends. Patients are simply choosing to stay out of the hospital and remain in their home or other setting, such as an assisted living or nursing home. When patients choose this option, they often enroll in home nursing or home hospice programs. Home care nurses continue monitoring their condition and provide necessary treatments. Patients and their families agree, however, that if their condition worsens, the person chooses to stay in a familiar place and treat the disease conservatively rather than with the full array of medical interventions available in the hospital. As with DNR/DNI orders, patients or their health care proxies can always change their minds. Just saying the word will reverse the order and the patient will go to the hospital.

HOSPICE CARE

In the final stages of most terminal illnesses, patients lose weight and become increasingly weak. They may have needed hospitalization several times already, and in the case of heart or lung failure, they may have survived one or more flare-ups of their disease. At this point, patients and families often consider hospice as an alternative to the revolving door of hospitalization and the distressing prospect of continued struggle.

If a physician judges that a patient has a reasonable chance of passing away within six months, that patient is eligible for hospice care. Typically, hospice is covered by either Medicare or private insurance. When a patient enrolls in hospice, nurses and social workers begin to visit the patient where he or she lives, either at home or in a care facility.

In general, when patients enroll in hospice, they accept the terminal nature of their illness and choose to discontinue most life-prolonging treatments, focusing medical efforts instead on providing comfort. It's a subtle but important change in priorities: Traditional medical care focuses primarily on treating disease, whereas hospice focuses primarily on alleviating symptoms and discomfort. For instance, is it really important to treat diabetes with aggressive insulin and blood sugar monitoring when someone is in the final stages of cancer? It might be, if not doing so would lead to discomforts like frequent urination or thirst. However, if being poked with syringes eight times daily wouldn't help someone feel better, it would probably be more humane to stop. Hospice programs will help ensure that your loved one is taking medications that provide maximal comfort and possibly discontinue burdensome or unnecessary treatments.

Recently, a few home hospice agencies have begun providing elements of medical care not typically offered by hospice, such as blood transfusions, IV nutrition, and certain types of chemotherapy. Sometimes patients with specific insurance coverage can enroll in hospice while continuing aggressive, disease-focused care with the purpose of prolonging life. It's important to know that this type of care, called *open access* hospice, is still rare. For this reason, we've chosen to focus on traditional hospice services in this book.

Despite hospice's focus on maximizing comfort rather than providing life-prolonging treatments, enrolling in hospice by no means guarantees that death will come within six months. Although some patients in hospice may pass away sooner than those receiving life-prolonging treatments, when exactly a patient will pass away is always uncertain. Surprisingly, recent research demonstrates that for heart failure and some forms of cancer, patients may actually live longer in hospice compared to traditional care (Connor et al. 2007). For many others, hospital care provides no improvement in either their life span or the quality of their remaining time (Fisher et al. 2003).

As patients enrolled in hospice care near death, they typically choose to stay where they are, rather than transfer to a hospital. This is often a challenging concept for patients and families who have grown accustomed to sudden trips to the emergency room and lengthy hospital stays. Whereas before the patient may have gone to the hospital for tests when symptoms worsened, the same symptoms now might prompt a call to the hospice nurse. As we've discussed, many patients will experience repeated exacerbations of their illnesses. Enrolling in hospice means accepting that the next flare-up could be the final one. People often fear that death will be a painful and traumatic event. Luckily, with hospice care this is rarely the case. Hospice providers work hard to keep such worst-case scenarios from occurring.

For more information on hospice, be sure to read chapter 5. In addition, we recommend two excellent books: *The Hospice Choice*, by Marcia Lattanzi-Licht, John Mahoney, and Galen Miller (1998), and *The Hospice Handbook*, by Larry Beresford (1993). If you and your loved one are considering hospice, the information in these books will make an excellent complement to the guidance found within this book.

WHAT'S THE RIGHT DECISION?

After reading this chapter, you may find yourself asking, "What's the right thing to do?" Most of the time, there is no single right treatment to choose. Doctors can tell you what options are available, but it's likely that you and your loved one will still face difficult choices. It's easy to get bogged down in the details of all the care options outlined in this chapter. Keep in mind that decisions made at the end of life are intensely personal. Whatever choices are ultimately made, they should be consistent with your loved one's wishes and values.

CHAPTER 4

What Can I Do About My Loved One's Pain and Suffering?

Addressing Symptoms and Difficulties

Amy's father, Richard, had always been a tough son of a gun. He fought in Korea, put in twenty-nine solid years as a machinist, and had endured excruciating back pain for most of his life. But when prostate cancer quickly spread throughout his body, Richard's life changed dramatically. The things he used to take for granted as part of his active lifestyle were now insurmountable challenges. Still, he managed to go on monthly forays to the beach with his daughter. Something about the sand, the surf, the children frolicking—it took his mind away from the pain and the slow passage of time. For this reason, neither Richard nor his daughter were prepared for the difficult conversation that was about to take place.

"Sweetheart," sighed Richard as he leaned on his new walker, "I'm not sure I'm up for the beach today."

Amy braced herself against the kitchen table, holding back tears and wishing she hadn't heard those words. "Why, Dad? We don't have to go for that long."

"Amy, it's just too much. Getting in the car, walking down from the parking lot to the sand, setting up the chairs—I just don't feel like I can do it anymore."

Grasping for any possible solution, Amy asked, "What is it, Dad? Are you too tired? Are you hurting? Dr. Lane gave you more pills for the pain."

"I am tired, Sweetie," said Richard, "but really, sometimes it just hurts too much. The pills make me feel lousy. If I'm not in pain, then I'm queasy. My guts hurt. I have to pee all the time, and it hurts to get up and even try to use the bathroom. I'll miss the beach, and I'll miss being there with you. I really hope we can go again, but not today."

SOMETIMES IT JUST HURTS TOO MUCH

People coping with life-threatening and terminal illnesses must confront a variety of issues. Many of the chapters in this book contain strategies for addressing emotional and spiritual struggles. But as dying people consider these deeper issues, they also face incredible physical challenges that impair their ability to enjoy the final months of life: pain, nausea, breathlessness, and other distressing symptoms. You and your loved one may understandably fear these symptoms more than dying itself. Fortunately, good medical care can help improve these problems dramatically, allowing your loved one to live out life's final stages with as much satisfaction as possible. Ultimately, Richard may lose the energy and independence required to venture to the beach, but pain should never hinder having a meaningful connection with his daughter. In this chapter, we'll discuss a number of the symptoms associated with chronic and terminal illnesses, as well as strategies that can be used to minimize their impact.

PAIN AND PAIN CONTROL

Pain is the symptom most feared by people who are dying and those who love them. We frequently hear patients say, "I'm not afraid of dying, but I am afraid of the pain." If your loved one already has experienced significant pain, you know that it can affect virtually every aspect of life. People in pain often have difficulty functioning, don't feel like doing things they normally find pleasurable, and can wind up feeling helpless or even depressed. Fortunately, an enormous arsenal of pain medicines and other treatments can be used to help minimize suffering as disease worsens. While it's rarely possible to eliminate pain entirely, it's hardly ever true that "nothing more can be done."

In the next few pages, we'll discuss some of the treatments available for pain and how to utilize them effectively. Of course, because medical technology is always progressing, be sure to ask your loved one's doctor for updated information.

Over-the-Counter Pain Medications

Most people are very familiar with over-the-counter medications like Tylenol (acetaminophen) and Motrin (ibuprofen), and have access to them without visiting a doctor. Just because these drugs are easily available, however, doesn't mean they're guaranteed to be safe. Don't use more than the dose suggested on the bottle unless recommended by a doctor.

Acetaminophen is readily available without a prescription. One of the reasons that acetaminophen is so attractive is that it rarely produces significant side effects. For instance, it's unlikely to cause drowsiness or nausea. For mild pain, acetaminophen alone is often sufficient for adequate pain control. If your loved one has more advanced disease, however, it probably won't provide enough relief. Although it's tempting to take more acetaminophen as pain worsens, patients must be careful not to consume beyond a certain amount. Typically, doctors recommend taking less than four grams daily, sometimes even less if patients have liver disease. That means no more than eight extra-strength Tylenol (or the equivalent) per day.

Medications like ibuprofen (Motrin, Advil) and naproxen sodium (Aleve) are in another category of readily available pain medications. These nonsteroidal anti-inflammatory drugs, often referred to as NSAIDs, are a bit stronger than acetaminophen and are very helpful for pain caused by inflammation, particularly from cancer that has spread to the bones. Using them regularly can help reduce your loved one's need for other types of pain medicines, thereby lowering the risk of side effects. Unfortunately, they can cause stomach irritation or bleeding and possibly kidney damage. Although NSAIDs do have side effects, it's important to keep your loved one's goals in mind. A long-term risk of kidney damage is probably not the most important concern if your loved one has only a very limited time to live. In this case, quick and effective pain relief may be a lot more important. As always, a doctor can help you and your loved one balance the burdens of a medication with the benefits.

When Over-the-Counter Pain Medications Don't Work

Patients suffering from pain often first try over-the-counter medications because they're easily available. Although this frequently works for a while, most patients with advanced illness eventually find that these medications alone aren't enough. If this is the case for your loved one, you should speak to the doctor about it as soon as possible. Although many patients and families fear that the only choice is to accept and endure the pain, in reality there are many good options still available. For instance, the doctor might prescribe a higher dose of an over-the-counter medication that your loved one already is taking. If pain continues to worsen, however, the doctor may suggest one of several opiate pain relievers.

Morphine and Other Opiate Pain Medications

Opiate medications are usually reserved for more severe pain, typically when over-the-counter medications have failed to relieve pain adequately. Unfortunately, they come with a somewhat undeserved bad reputation—patients and families often fear them out of concerns about severe sedation or addiction. When prescribed and managed effectively, it's usually possible to get good pain relief without confusion or excessive sleepiness. Also, for patients responsibly taking morphine or other opiates as prescribed by a physician, true addiction is rare. As your loved one's illness worsens, increasing amounts of pain medication may be needed, but this doesn't mean that your loved one is addicted. Taking more medication because the pain is worse isn't the same as addiction. When taken under proper medical supervision, this is often an appropriate and necessary strategy.

Opiate pain relievers are a critical part of managing the pain caused by cancer or organ failure, and they shouldn't be avoided out of fear. As always, ask your loved one's doctor if you have specific concerns or questions. In reality, sometimes pain is so severe that high doses of opiate pain relievers are necessary, and the side effects of sleepiness and confusion are unavoidable. If this is occurring, it's important to consider your loved one's goals: Would he or she prefer to be awake and mentally sharp but in pain, or sleepy yet physically comfortable? There is no right or wrong decision here. Different people and different situations call for different choices. Thankfully, this dilemma presents itself less commonly than most people think.

If your loved one is considering or currently taking opiate pain medications and you would like more information about them, the following descriptions may help answer some of your questions.

COMBINATION DRUGS

Some medications, like Vicodin, Norco, and Percocet, are combinations of acetaminophen and a relatively mild opiate painkiller. They are often the first medications physicians turn to for pain relief when over-the-counter drugs aren't enough. Because acetaminophen can cause liver damage when taken too often, these medications can only be used in limited doses. If patients need the medication more frequently, it's often time to consider other treatment options. It's all too common for patients to rely on increasing doses of combination drugs even when they're clearly not working. If this is the case for your loved one, don't be afraid to ask the doctor about other strategies.

STRONGER OPIATE MEDICATIONS

Among the stronger opiate pain relievers, morphine is the best known. It works well for most patients and is often the medication of choice because of its effectiveness and relatively low cost. Nonetheless, there are many additional opiate pain medications, such as oxycodone (Oxycontin), hydromorphone (Dilaudid), fentanyl (Duragesic), and methadone (Dolophine), among others. Some are long-lasting and help dull pain for hours, while others rapidly relieve pain for a briefer period of time. Some come in pill form and others are injectable; fentanyl even comes in a patch and a lollipop.

True allergies to any opiate are extraordinarily rare; most often when patients complain of allergies, they're really experiencing side effects. When starting any opiate, for instance, patients may notice nausea or mild sedation, though these symptoms almost always go away within a few days. All opiates also can cause constipation, which we'll discuss in detail later in the chapter.

Interventional Pain Management

In some cases, your loved one's doctor may call upon a colleague to provide assistance with pain relief. Anesthesiologists and other specialists in interventional pain management can sometimes offer strategies that maximize pain relief while minimizing the side effects of medicines. For instance, by using a nerve block, these physicians may be able to deaden sensitive nerves irritated by a spreading cancer. Painful joints can be injected with medications to reduce discomfort and inflammation. Also, specialists in pain management can place small catheters, which are somewhat like IV lines, near the spinal cord to deliver medication to dull pain in the body. This puts medication right where pain is transmitted, thereby causing fewer side effects in comparison to traditional medicines that act on many parts of the body at once. When people are suffering severe side effects from more traditional pain medications, it's often reasonable to ask about approaches like these.

Nonmedical Approaches to Pain Management

Many nonmedical techniques can be used alongside traditional approaches to help relieve pain. Massage therapy, acupuncture and acupressure, biofeedback, guided imagery, hypnotherapy, and other psychological approaches often work wonders, typically causing far fewer side effects and worries than medications. You may wonder whether these alternative approaches are appropriate for your loved one. Don't be afraid to ask your loved one's doctor. Most physicians are open to such approaches as long as they don't interfere with traditional treatments. In fact, many hospitals provide these services or can refer you to centers that do.

A combination of the medications and approaches mentioned above almost always can provide reasonable pain control. It may not be possible to conquer pain entirely, as some discomfort is always part of serious illness. But pain should never sap all the enjoyment out of life or dominate someone's life completely. Don't be afraid to raise the issue of untreated pain and ask about alternative medications or approaches. The next exercise will help you dialogue with your loved one's doctor more effectively.

EXERCISE
Talking with the Doctor About Pain

The most important job of patients and their families is to keep the doctor well-informed. Pain can't be treated unless the doctor first knows about it! Generally, physicians will want to know where the pain is located, what it feels like, how long it has lasted, when it typically occurs, and how severe it is. Consider jotting down answers to the following questions in your notebook. You then can use these notes to communicate as precisely as possible with the doctor.

- ■ Where is the pain? Describe as precisely as possible where the pain seems to be located. If it's in more than one place, be sure to note this.

- ■ What does the pain feel like? Consider words like sharp, dull, throbbing, stinging, stabbing, tingling, or burning.

- ■ When did the pain begin?

- ■ When does the pain occur? Consider whether the pain typically occurs at a particular time of day.

- ■ Does anything make the pain worse? Consider whether the pain typically worsens when doing particular activities.

- ■ How bad is the pain? Although you can feel free to describe this in plain English, it's often more precise to give a numerical rating. Using the scale below, your loved one can pick out which number best describes the intensity of the pain.

0	1	2	3	4	5	6	7	8	9	10
none		mild			moderate				worst imaginable	

NAUSEA

Nausea and vomiting can be tremendously debilitating symptoms. It's truly miserable to feel nauseated all the time. If your loved one is experiencing nausea, it may come from one or more sources.

Nausea Caused by Chemotherapy

If your loved one is undergoing chemotherapy, you rightfully may be concerned about nausea. Thankfully, this symptom is becoming increasingly rare as new chemotherapy medications with fewer side effects are developed. Additionally, doctors' ability to prevent and treat chemotherapy-induced nausea is improving every day. When a patient is undergoing chemotherapy, oncologists usually give antinausea drugs known as antiemetics. These medications generally work well, though they sometimes cause side effects like sedation. There are other medical options as well. For instance, if inflammation in the gut is causing your loved one to feel nauseous, the doctor may recommend an injection of a steroid medication.

Finally, some patients experience anticipatory nausea, meaning that the feeling of nausea begins even before they receive chemotherapy medications. This may be the result of anxiety. Chemotherapy can be stressful, especially when someone expects to feel very nauseated afterward. In this case, antianxiety medications may help. Additionally, sometimes it helps to engage in activities that distract focus from the chemotherapy. On the way to the clinic, for instance, you can help your loved one by making conversation about an engaging topic or tuning the radio to a favorite channel. Some patients also report that relaxation or breathing exercises help. Tapes containing such exercises can be found in many music stores and bookstores.

Nausea Caused by Opiate Pain Medications

As mentioned previously, opiate pain relievers like morphine can sometimes cause nausea. One side effect of these medications is that they slow down activity in the stomach and intestines, keeping food and liquid in the stomach for too long. Fortunately, if this is the case for your loved one, the nausea probably will go away within a few days of starting the opiate as the body adjusts to the medication. Opiates can also cause constipation, which in turn can lead to nausea; we'll address this in the next section.

There's no reason for your loved one to feel terribly nauseous, even for a short time. Doctors often can prescribe medication to speed up the gut again, providing relief. Other medications work directly on the brain to help reduce the feeling of nausea. The most important point is that nausea from pain medication should never prevent good pain control. If the first thing you try doesn't work, keep asking the physician for help. The doctor should be able to find a combination of medications or strategies that both controls pain and keeps nausea in check.

Nausea Caused by Constipation

When patients are chronically ill, constipation is relatively common. When people are not eating and drinking as much as previously, dehydration and constipation often follow. Plus, many medications needed at the end of life—painkillers, antidepressants, and even nausea medications—can cause or worsen constipation. Unfortunately, this quite often leads to nausea. If you believe that your loved one's constipation is caused by a particular medicine, be sure to tell the doctor. When possible, the doctor will stop any problematic medications. Sometimes medications that cause constipation are necessary to treat other symptoms and can't be stopped. In these cases, the doctor will try to treat the constipation in other ways. We'll discuss strategies for doing this later in the chapter.

Nausea Caused by Bowel Obstruction

A final possible cause of nausea occurs when tumors push on the intestines, causing a bowel obstruction. When this happens, patients can feel bloated and nauseated, and they often vomit. Depending on the size and location of the cancer, obstruction can be either partial or complete. Partial bowel obstructions sometimes improve by avoiding eating or drinking for a few days. If this bowel rest strategy is successful, patients can often begin eating again. Before trying this, of course, be sure to consult with your loved one's doctor.

Complete obstructions are more challenging to treat. If pressure from a tumor completely closes off the gut, doctors may consider placing a tube through the nose down into the stomach to empty out air and fluids. Because this procedure is very uncomfortable for most patients, it's only a temporary solution. In some cases, doctors also will prescribe medications to reduce swelling around a tumor, taking some of the pressure off. If these strategies don't relieve the problem, physicians may suggest a stent, which involves inserting a tube inside the gut to prop a passageway open. Alternatively, they may suggest a venting gastrostomy, which involves placing a tube into the stomach directly though the skin. Food and liquid can then be emptied out of this tube, often relieving the symptoms. Although these procedures may seem drastic, they can lead to great relief for many patients.

SHORTNESS OF BREATH

Breathing is perhaps the most natural thing we do. Normally, we breathe without effort—and without even thinking about it. So, when we have trouble breathing, it can be unpleasant and provoke anxiety. Unfortunately, some terminal illnesses can cause chronic shortness of breath, known by the medical term dyspnea. People who suffer from dyspnea often fear that in their final weeks they literally will suffocate. If this is the case for your loved one, it's important to know that doctors can aggressively and successfully treat shortness of breath. No one should fear this kind of death.

People with chronic conditions like heart failure or chronic obstructive pulmonary disease (COPD) have probably already been taking medications to relieve breathlessness for quite some time. Even when a patient has decided to enroll in hospice or to avoid the hospital at all costs, it can be vitally important to continue these medications at home. If your loved one has heart failure, for instance, the doctor will probably recommend continuing diuretics like furosemide (Lasix) and other normal medications for as long as your loved one can take the pills. Patients with COPD usually continue using their inhalers until it's quite clear that they're not helping anymore. If these measures alone don't work satisfactorily, doctors may prescribe the very same opiates that they employ against pain. These medications work to expand the arteries in the lungs, easing the passage of oxygen and lessening the feeling of breathlessness.

Using an oxygen tank sometimes also helps relieve shortness of breath, though this isn't always the case. A person can have perfectly healthy levels of oxygen in the body and still have a feeling of breathlessness. The measure of oxygen saturation (the amount of oxygen in the blood) can captivate family members; they often hang onto the number, riding an emotional roller coaster when it dips or peaks. In our experience, however, it's much more important to ask whether the patient feels short of breath. Even when oxygen saturation stays low, a steady flow of supplemental oxygen or even a gentle breeze may improve the uncomfortable sensation of breathlessness.

CONSTIPATION

People suffering from chronic and terminal diseases often notice that they're less able to stay regular. As illness worsens, the gut frequently slows down. Medications for pain, breathlessness, and depression also can worsen constipation. Decreased intake of food and water can complicate the situation still further. Patients may experience abdominal pain and cramps and find themselves straining to have bowel movements.

It's important to understand that bowel movements naturally decrease when someone has chronic illness. Less frequent bowel movements may not require any treatment at all, especially if they're not causing pain, nausea, or other discomfort. Still, with constipation an ounce of prevention is definitely worth a pound of cure. Keeping it from happening is always the best option. For instance, if your loved one is taking opiate pain medications, you should be sure to ask the doctor about starting a medicine to ward off constipation.

If constipation does occur, seriously ill patients often require more aggressive laxatives, either by mouth or in the form of enemas or suppositories, to get things moving again. This can cause diarrhea or cramping temporarily, but it's usually worth it to prevent pain and suffering down the road. After the constipation is relieved, patients most often return to more simple, preventative measures.

Many patients and family members find it annoying that nurses and doctors seem to constantly be asking about bowel movements. We remember one eighty-five-year-old patient who became extremely embarrassed when she was asked about a recent bowel movement in front of her daughter. However, if someone hasn't had a bowel movement in several days and develops stomach pains, cramps, or diarrhea, the constipation may have turned into an impaction. This occurs when stool hardens in the intestine, blocking everything behind it. This can be a painful medical emergency. Let the doctor know if you think this is occurring, because it's always better to handle impaction early.

URINARY ISSUES

As with constipation, people nearing the end of life often have trouble with urination. They may need to urinate so frequently that it's troubling, especially when getting out of bed is difficult. Other times, medications needed for pain, depression, or high blood pressure can cause them to have difficulty urinating even though their bladder is full. Both of these problems can result from urinary retention, a condition in which the body has difficulty expelling a sufficient amount of urine. Sometimes doctors may be able to remove the medications causing the problem, but other times they're just too crucial to stop.

A common solution to urinary problems is to use a foley catheter. This involves placing a tube through the urethra directly into the bladder; urine then empties into a bag that can be managed either in the hospital or at home. If you're like most people, the thought of this procedure seems unpleasant at best. Nonetheless, not having to struggle to the bathroom or use a bedpan is a great relief to many patients.

One of the most troubling effects of urinary difficulty is the embarrassment and loss of dignity that some patients feel. Your loved one may have spent his or her lifetime building a strong and independent sense of self. He or she may boast impressive accomplishments or may have helped count-less people. Given this history, it's not easy to accept the reality of needing help to use the restroom. People in this position often worry that they are burdening their family and friends with unpleasant tasks. In our experience, however, caregivers frequently look at the situation quite differently. Many people welcome the opportunity to give back to someone they love. Although helping a loved one is often difficult physically and emotionally, it also can be personally meaningful and even therapeutic. If you feel this way, sharing your feelings with your loved one is often very comforting.

DEHYDRATION

Dehydration and thirst are common in patients confronting terminal illness. Dehydration often results from the disease itself combined with a decreased intake of liquids. When this occurs, thirst sometimes follows. But while dehydration is fairly universal at the end of life, thirst and hunger aren't. Correcting dehydration by delivering fluids through an IV line can sometimes improve symptoms such as confusion or shaking, and it may even prolong life. However, IV fluids might not significantly improve quality of life, as they often create swelling in the legs or abdomen and can extend the dying process inappropriately. Patients and families should ask themselves and their physician whether IV fluids are helping to improve quality of life or simply prolonging suffering. For someone who is termi-nally ill, the burden of coming to the hospital or clinic for IV fluids also may override any real benefits. Nonetheless, it's sometimes worth trying IV fluids. If problems arise, you and your loved one can determine whether it's worth it to continue.

First, however, it's important to separate true dehydration from the feelings of thirst and dry mouth. While dehydration may be improved when fluids are delivered through an IV line, thirst and dry mouth might not. This is because these symptoms frequently come from other sources. For instance, thirst and dry mouth can be a side effect of common medi-cations such as blood pressure pills, pain relievers, and antinausea drugs. Unfortunately, medications that cause thirst and dry mouth often are necessary and can't be stopped without other symptoms worsening, so other solutions are sometimes necessary.

One of the most effective solutions is surprisingly simple. If your loved one is experiencing thirst, your first urge may be to encourage him or her to drink more. Unfortunately, this can be an unpleasant experience for patients with difficulty swallowing. If your loved one can't take in a great deal of fluid, swabbing the inside of the mouth with a moist sponge can greatly improve dry mouth and the sensation of thirst. To feel better, many people just need to "wet their whistle" rather than receive IV fluids or drink many cups of water.

FEAR OF PAIN AND SUFFERING

Perhaps the worst result of symptoms like the ones discussed in this chapter is the fear that they'll get worse. Although discomfort is an inevitable part of serious illness, it need not prevent your loved one from spending the last chapter of life in a satisfying and meaningful way. As long as patients and their families keep doctors well-informed, there are numerous tools for treating almost any symptom that rears its ugly head. With proper medical attention, not only can symptoms usually be reduced, but so can the fear that often accompanies them.

CHAPTER 5

Where Will It Happen?

Choosing the Right Place for Your Loved One

Sophie had been in the hospital for three weeks, and nothing was working. With the unflinching support of her daughter, Marie, she had battled breast cancer for over six years. Now it was clear that the battle was almost over.

Even after this realization, there were still many complicated decisions to be made. Sophie had wanted to try everything to fight the cancer, even if the odds of success were low. Having survived World War II living in Warsaw, she was fond of saying that nothing could scare her. Her tolerance for suffering was great, and she usually hid her pain well. Nonetheless, Marie could tell that her mother was definitely suffering. The last course of chemotherapy had almost killed her; she barely beat a horrible pneumonia that resulted from her weakened immune system. After that experience, her doctors recommended comfort care, and Sophie reluctantly accepted. No more chemotherapy, no more blood draws, no more trips to the intensive care unit.

"Now that she's receiving comfort care," a young medical resident said to Marie, "we'll need to move her to a nursing home."

"I don't want her moving anywhere," said Marie. "She's moved enough."

"We'd love to keep her here," said her oncologist, Dr. Myers, "but the hospital needs the bed. Hospitals are for people who have a good chance of getting better."

"You told me you would keep her comfortable. She's comfortable here. Why can't she just stay?" implored Marie.

"When we moved her from intensive care," said the resident, "we didn't think she'd live more than a day or so. Now she's stabilized, and she might live for a few more weeks. We don't really know. You might want to think about taking her home or finding a good hospice. I'm sure you can find the right place for her."

"I can't take her home," cried Marie. "I've got three kids, a husband, and a job that I've been missing too much of. She's safe here. She knows everyone. This is the right place for her. After all that she's gone through, you want me to move her to some strange place to die?"

The two doctors looked at each other nervously, but neither could come up with any words for Marie or her mother.

Marie looked down at her feet and shook her head in despair and disgust. "If she's sick enough to be dying, why isn't she sick enough to stay in the hospital?"

THE RIGHT PLACE

If your family is like most, you wrestle with the question of where your loved one should spend the last chapter of life. In past decades, patients nearing the end of life usually checked into the hospital. Sometimes this decision was driven by the hope of temporary improvement. Other times, they didn't have a support system at home that could provide comfort and security. People saw the hospital as a place of refuge at the time of death. Today, as hospitals become more crowded and less able to accommodate dying patients, this situation has changed dramatically. In most cases, if dying patients are relatively stable, they must find an alternative place to stay.

If you've confronted this issue, you know that it's not always clear which place is right for your loved one. If your family has the financial and social resources to make dying at home possible, you're fortunate. Other options include nursing homes or other forms of inpatient care. Unfortunately, a great many people with terminal illness and their families never seriously consider where the death should take place. Without a plan, patients often bounce between the hospital and home until they're close enough to death that the hospital can't responsibly discharge them. This process can be extremely stressful for everyone. In our experience, however, if families are well-informed and carefully consider the options, they can avoid many difficulties. In the next few pages, we'll offer information about some of the options that may be available to your loved one. By considering the pros and cons of each, you and your loved one will be able to make the best decision possible.

In the Hospital

According to recent national statistics, about half of all patients with chronic illness die in the hospital (Teno 2001). Most of these deaths are unplanned but not totally unexpected. Many seriously ill patients enter the hospital with the hope of feeling better and leaving, even though their doctors may have said otherwise. When patients are believed to be dying, hospitals often provide a type of treatment known as comfort care. In other words, when efforts to reverse an illness have failed, doctors often recommend focusing efforts on providing comfort rather than cure. This might involve any of the following:

- Stopping medications that don't directly provide comfort, including treatments exclusively focused on prolonging life.

- Stopping or reducing the number of blood draws and other tests.

- Minimizing intravenous (IV) fluids and artificial nutrition.

- Discontinuation of life support measures like ventilators or dialysis.

- Increasing treatment of pain, shortness of breath, and other uncomfortable symptoms.

- Transfer to a private room in the hospital or to a specialized inpatient unit for dying patients.

All people, even doctors, are poor at predicting when people will die. That said, doctors generally suggest comfort care when they believe that a patient has only hours or days left to live. When a dying patient is likely to live somewhat longer, doctors may instead direct the conversation toward hospice care, which we'll discuss later in this chapter.

There are advantages and disadvantages to spending the last days of life in the hospital. In most cases, hospitals possess greater technological capabilities than other settings. Most hospitalized patients have IV lines in place, allowing nurses to administer medications without the patient having to swallow anything or use a suppository. In addition, hospitals generally provide more nursing support than a nursing home or hospice. Certain terminal illnesses are very complicated and may require greater expertise, medication, and equipment than is typically available at home or in a nursing facility. Frequently, however, the most significant advantage of the hospital is the psychological reassurance it provides. For many patients and families, having trained physicians and nurses quickly available outweighs any disadvantages.

On the other hand, the hospital can be a very unpleasant place to die. Hospitals exist primarily to cure disease and prolong life. At the time of death, this is rarely possible. Trying to halt an inevitable process of dying sometimes results in prolonged or even increased suffering. Doctors and nurses can focus so intently on prolonging life that they don't adequately attend to the patient's other needs—pain control, symptom management, and emotional support. They may perform painful tests and provide irrelevant treatments that ultimately don't lead to greater comfort. It's hard to criticize these impulses, because at other times they save countless lives. Unfortunately, the intensive treatment characteristic of most hospitals may not be appropriate when someone is dying. For this reason, many people choose to die at home, where they and their families can have greater control over the process.

Fortunately, some hospitals have services or units dedicated to patients who are suffering from chronic and advanced illnesses. Hospitals increasingly employ physicians, nurses, and other professionals who specialize in palliative care. Like comfort care, palliative care focuses on reducing symptoms and increasing comfort. However, palliative care differs from comfort care in that patients sometimes continue to receive life-prolonging treatments like chemotherapy, radiation, and even surgery. Because palliative care is a relatively new medical discipline, trained experts might not be available in all areas. Nonetheless, it's worth asking if palliative care services exist at your loved one's hospital. They can be tremendously useful in helping achieve physical comfort and improve the family's understanding of the illness process.

In a Nursing Home

For roughly a quarter of the people in the United States, a nursing home is the final place they receive care (Teno 2001). In recent years, nursing homes have become a more common place to pass away. As medical technology advances and families separate, it's becoming more and more complicated for families to manage serious illness at home. As a result, more and more families are turning to nursing homes.

Like hospitals, nursing homes have advantages and disadvantages. While not staffed to the level of a hospital, nursing homes feature twenty-four-hour nursing staff and may have an on-site physician. Some nursing homes also can administer IV medications, which are necessary for certain patients. Additionally, there are usually nurse assistants available to handle cleaning, bathing, and other aspects of daily care, sparing families this responsibility.

The cost of a nursing home is probably its biggest disadvantage. Only a small number of people purchase long-term care insurance, which can pay for such facilities. Unfortunately, because many of these policies have waiver periods of up to six months from the time of purchase, they need to be bought early. Without long-term care insurance, nursing homes can be brutally expensive. This can be a crushing burden for the average family.

The fact that nursing home care for the dying isn't paid for by Medicare or most standard medical insurance policies often confuses people. For specific information about what's covered, it's always a good idea to check your loved one's particular insurance policy. In general, however, Medicare and insurance companies make a distinction between skilled care and custodial care. Skilled care, consisting of technically complex procedures like complicated wound management, IV antibiotics, and physical therapy, is often covered. In cases where this type of care is needed by a dying patient, Medicare and medical insurance may pay for this. More often, however, care for terminally ill people is considered custodial and isn't covered financially. No one would argue that care for dying people is unskilled. But it's not skilled in the way that these policies require for funding.

There are a couple of important exceptions to this financial rule. First, if your loved one is an honorably discharged U.S. veteran, he or she may qualify for admission to a Veterans Affairs (VA) nursing home or hospice care center. For more information, contact the Department of Veterans Affairs (800-827-1000; www.va.gov). Second, for extremely low-income patients, federal and state Medicaid may provide basic care in a nursing home. To see whether this is an option for your loved one, contact the Centers for Medicare and Medicaid Services (800-633-4227; www.cms. hhs.gov). Most patients and families, however, are forced to dip into savings to pay for end-of-life custodial care.

It's important to know that nursing homes have varying levels of comfort in handling dying patients. When they believe that a patient is dying, the staff of some nursing homes will automatically dial 911 and rush the patient to the hospital by ambulance. This can be disturbing to families who have consciously chosen not to care for their loved one in the hospital. If you're considering a nursing home, be sure to discuss this issue in advance. Many terminally ill patients invoke a do not rehospitalize order (see chapter 3) in order to make their preference on this matter clear. In addition, patients in most nursing facilities can enroll in home hospice programs. This means that nurses and social workers from a separate hospice agency will visit the patient as if in a private home. Their expertise in caring for dying patients can be as much a comfort to nursing home staff as to patients and families. We'll discuss home hospice care in greater detail later in the chapter.

In an Inpatient Hospice

Some communities have inpatient hospices available to people approaching the end of life. Even the most loving families can have intense difficulty caring for a dying person at home. We've heard many family members say that they feel more like nurses than husbands, wives, sisters, brothers, sons, or daughters. Like nursing homes, inpatient hospice facilities provide family members freedom from the heavy burden of moment-to-moment caregiving. Many patients also prefer having professional caregivers, rather than family members, performing these chores.

More than nursing homes, inpatient hospices offer services geared toward handling the dying process in all of its complexity—from nurses and doctors trained in the skilled management of physical symptoms to social workers and chaplains who can provide the emotional counseling that patients and families often require. After the death, they may even provide bereavement support. Sadly, in many communities, there are fewer hospice beds than needed. Moreover, physicians don't always know where and when beds are available. For more information about the availability of hospice services in your area, contact the National Hospice and Palliative Care Organization (800-658-8898; www.nhpco.org). Another good option is to ask a social worker in the hospital where your loved one has received care; this person can help you and your loved one decide on the best place to be. Also, if you haven't already, be sure to read chapter 3 for more information about the type of care provided by inpatient and home hospice services.

As with nursing homes, Medicare and private insurance rarely cover the cost of inpatient hospice. Fortunately, many inpatient hospices are supported by charity, making them less costly than most nursing homes. In addition, the Veterans Affairs system provides inpatient hospice care to most honorably discharged U.S. veterans. To secure a hospice bed, it helps to have received care at the VA previously, but it isn't required. If your loved one served in the U.S. armed forces, contact the Department of Veterans Affairs for more information (for contact information, see the section on nursing homes above).

At Home

Most people express a wish to die in the comfort of their own homes. As noted physician Walter Bortz eloquently put it, "I hereby assert that when my end is at hand, I wish to have no pain, no tubes, and be at home with those I love" (2001, 135). Still, only about a quarter of people actually achieve this end (Teno 2001). Of course, like the other options discussed in this chapter, staying at home has both pros and cons.

There are many advantages. Rather than waiting for a nurse who is busy taking care of others, patients can take medications on their own schedules. Also, the interruptions and inconveniences of the hospital are avoided—no more middle-of-the-night vital signs checks, restrictions on visiting hours, tussles over a shared television, or blare of a busy nursing station. Most importantly, being at home offers patients the comfort of a familiar place where they can find physical and spiritual calm.

Such advantages come at a price, however. Hiring caregivers to provide supervision and care quickly adds up financially, especially if care is needed twenty-four hours a day. And some people bristle at the idea of strangers in their house at any time, let alone a sensitive time like this. Consequently, the honor and struggle of caregiving often falls to family and friends.

Although many people have a network of family and friends who are both willing and able to shoulder this burden, others don't. It's often impossible for an elderly person to lift his or her spouse out of bed or perform any number of necessary tasks. And for patients with very complex physical problems, the greater technical expertise found in hospitals, nursing homes, and inpatient hospice facilities may be necessary.

Fortunately, home hospice provides an excellent alternative that makes it possible for many people to stay at home. Typically funded by Medicare or private insurance, home hospice programs provide nurses, home health aides, medical equipment, and medications for pain and other symptoms. Furthermore, social workers and chaplains are available for the patient and family's practical, emotional, and spiritual needs. Hospice nurses visit two to three times per week and can make emergency visits if necessary. They're also available by phone at any time and can instruct family and friends in proper care.

As mentioned earlier, if your loved one chooses to remain at home, you probably will need to take an active role in providing care. Even with the significant assistance of home hospice staff, however, you may wonder whether you'll be able to shoulder the burden. Late nights, early mornings, physical strain, and a roller coaster of emotions are not uncommon realities for caregivers. Although caregiving is often well worth the effort, you may understandably find yourself feeling burnt-out after a while. It's important to keep in mind that home hospice agencies rarely provide continuous care in the home or shoulder the cost of long-term placement in a facility. In the event that home care becomes impossible for any reason, hospice social workers can help you find an appropriate alternative placement. If the difficulty at home is likely to be temporary, they sometimes can arrange hospital, nursing home, or inpatient hospice respite stays for up to five days, then return care to you in the home setting.

In general, however, enrolling in hospice (whether home-based or inpatient) means that care will no longer take place in the hospital, an idea often difficult for both patients and families to accept. While the intrusions and discomforts of the hospital are many, if you're like most people, you think of the hospital as a provider of hope and longer life. Even when you've accepted that your loved one's illness is terminal, it can be excruciating to accept that the next big complication may be the final one. It may help to know that many patients experience not only better days with hospice, but more of them, too (Connor et al. 2007). Frequent ambulance rides to the hospital and long nights in the emergency room rarely improve anything for a patient in the final stages of terminal illness. Hospice helps maximize physical comfort and spares dying patients the rigors of an intensive care unit or the distress of dying in a strange place. Although philosophically it can be a difficult pill to swallow, hospice may have real advantages over hospital care at the end of life.

HOW TO DECIDE AMONG THE OPTIONS

Like many important decisions, there is no right or wrong answer to the question of where your loved one should spend the final chapter of life. Nonetheless, because this issue involves so many practical, medical, and emotional issues, it can seem overwhelming. In addition to considering the information in this chapter, we recommend leaning heavily on your loved one's physician or social worker. Because not all services are appropriate for all patients, these professionals can help clarify the situation and connect you with many of the resources discussed in this chapter.

EXERCISE
Considering the Pros and Cons

If a doctor or social worker isn't available to help with the decision about where your loved one will spend his or her final days, here is a simple exercise that may help organize your thoughts. First, take a moment to consider which care settings discussed in this chapter would be acceptable to you and your loved one. If your loved one is able, ask for his or her input. Perhaps you easily can identify one or more options as unsatisfactory at the moment. Now, open your notebook to a blank page. Along the left-hand side of the page, write down the options that are still on the table, with some space between them. Next, make two columns and label one "pros" and the other "cons."

The final step will require some work. For each of the settings you wrote down, reread that section of the chapter and jot down the pros and cons as you understand them. It may be that certain aspects of a particular setting would be pros to one person but cons to another. Just put them wherever they belong based on your understanding of your loved one's wishes. Now, take a look at the page. Which care setting has the most pros for your loved one? Which has the least cons? Does one setting appear to be clearly better to you? When speaking with your loved one's doctor or social worker, consider showing them this list. It may help to spark meaningful conversation about where your loved one will be most comfortable.

NO DECISION IS PERMANENT

It may be reassuring to know that no decision about where to live or what treatment to pursue is binding. If you and your loved one initially choose hospital care, this doesn't mean that hospice is off the table. Similarly, if you choose home hospice care, it's always possible to change course and seek life-prolonging care in the hospital. Whatever options are under consideration, we urge you to carefully consider how each one relates to your loved one's goals. Is it more important to remain home in a comfortable setting, or is there something to be gained by what a hospital or nursing home offers? Will the technological capabilities of a hospital help achieve a meaningful goal for your loved one, or will these resources simply prolong suffering? How does each option fit your loved one's basic values? Although grappling with these questions isn't easy, a little planning now can avoid great heartache later.

CHAPTER 6

How Will It Happen?

Dispelling Myths About the Final Days of Life

Henry had battled prostate cancer for eleven years. He always thought he would die of something else before the cancer. Maybe one of the kids he coached in basketball would give him a heart attack, he figured, or perhaps he would get a bad case of pneumonia like his wife had five years earlier. Almost a year ago, Dr. Logan even told him not to worry about the prostate cancer.

Since then, the cancer had spread to his bones. His back and hips ached constantly, though radiation therapy helped a little. He tried chemotherapy, but that hadn't worked out either. He felt sick and weak. As the months wore on, his appetite faded, he lost weight, and finally he took to his bed. His sister Lorraine moved in and began caring for him. She knew that Henry wanted to die at home and intended to help him fulfill this wish.

Lorraine made quick work of Henry's sitting room. She cleared out the furniture and moved the rented hospital bed in front of the television. She made phone calls to Henry's inner circle of friends, who in turn called some of Henry's former players, who then called other players. It seemed like hundreds of people came to visit! Although this pleased Henry, Lorraine sometimes had to turn people away when he couldn't take another well-wisher.

When the NCAA tournament started, Henry watched the games with dozens of the people whose lives he had touched. They sat at his side late into the night, cheering for upsets and exciting finishes. Lorraine kept the refrigerator full, and Henry made sure every plate had a generous helping of nachos.

By the tournament's final weekend, however, Henry's health had declined substantially. He could barely stay awake, and Lorraine almost decided to end the party. But Henry found great strength in the friends that kept arriving to honor him. During the final game, Henry slept, waking only to applause and screams.

When he passed away several days after the tournament's end, multiple generations of his players attended the funeral. After Lorraine spoke, there wasn't a dry eye in the church. "My brother Henry loved this community and loved his basketball," said Lorraine. "Henry died as he lived, surrounded by love, respect, and joy."

DYING IN CHARACTER

It's a common phrase among health care professionals: People die as they live. Although families often expect their loved ones to change dramatically or "see the light" as the end approaches, dying people rarely experience a change of personality or temperament. Quite the contrary: traits and idiosyncrasies frequently become more pronounced. The dying process seems to bring out who we are, for better or worse. Henry always derived strength and joy from those around him. This was no less true as he faced the final days and hours of life.

There are as many unique ways to face death as there are ways to live life. Your loved one may not cope with the situation the same way that you would. He or she may find personal peace and face the illness with grace—or not. Whether your loved one's final chapter is filled with calm or relative chaos, you should know that at the *very* end—the final hours or days—even the most disorganized and emotionally unhinged situations tend to settle down. Most deaths ultimately are peaceful. In this chapter, we'll discuss what you can expect as death draws near.

PHYSICAL CHANGES AT THE END OF LIFE

If you're like most people, you worry about what will happen to your loved one as death approaches. Naturally, many patients and families fear that death will be a dramatic event, filled with pain and suffering. In our experience, however, this fear is rarely realized. Rather, the dying process is more like a ship drifting out to sea, slowly and, generally, peacefully. Nonetheless, the body changes in a number of ways that can seem frightening if not properly understood. Family members often misinterpret these normal changes as signs of pain or distress. To help you prepare, we'll describe a number of these common changes.

One of the first things that many families notice is a lack of appetite. As the body begins to shut down, it doesn't require the amount of nutrition it once did. Initially, your loved one may get choosier about food. With time, his or her appetite may disappear completely. Ultimately, most patients stop eating and may even refuse fluids. If you're like most people, this transition won't be easy to witness. Many family members fear that their loved one is hungry or thirsty. It's important to realize, however, that decreased intake of food and water is generally quite natural and probably isn't uncomfortable for your loved one. If your loved one is able to swallow and wishes to eat a little, it's a good idea to have some snacks on hand. It's important, however, to fight the urge to push food and water. This may do little more than create discomfort.

You also may notice a change in breathing. Your loved one may take large gasps followed by long pauses, particularly during the last hours of life. You might even think that your loved one has died only to watch him or her take another big breath. Breathing may simply slow down over time until the pauses seem more frequent or longer than the breaths. These are natural changes and typically don't cause any discomfort. On the other hand, if your loved one appears to be heaving while breathing or is taking frequent short and shallow breaths, this could signify distress or discomfort. As we discussed in chapter 4, many medications are available to ease suffering at the end of life. Don't hesitate to report your observations to a nurse or doctor.

One very common symptom in the final stages of life is moist breathing, often referred to by the frightening term "death rattle." This unpleasant sound often alarms families, who worry that it may be a sign of pneumonia. The explanation is usually a lot simpler. As the mind separates from the body, people forget to swallow. Because the salivary glands keep making saliva, much of it remains in the back of the throat, producing a rattling or gurgling sound when a person breathes. Although moist breathing is probably not uncomfortable for your loved one, nurses can usually provide medications to help resolve it. You can also raise or lower the head of the bed if you feel that this would be more comfortable for your loved one.

Changes in skin color and temperature also are common as death approaches. You may notice that your loved one's skin is discolored during the final hours of life, appearing darker or blotchy. His or her body, particularly the hands, legs, and feet, may become increasingly cool to the touch. If this occurs, a warm blanket or two can help keep your loved one comfortable.

Some people become restless or agitated in the days leading up to death. Occasionally this restlessness persists until close to the end. Doctors can prescribe medications to calm such agitation, although reassuring words and a gentle touch may do just as much good. At times, you might also notice that your loved one moans. Be careful not to automatically interpret this as a sign of pain or distress. Sometimes this is a natural result of air passing over the vocal cords. Of course, if moaning occurs during movements, like cleaning or physical examination, doctors and nurses should consider the possibility that your loved one is in pain. Grimacing or withdrawal when being touched also can signify pain and may prompt health care providers to increase dosages of pain medication.

Ultimately, physical signs at the end of life can confuse even the most careful observer. If you have questions or concerns about what's happening to your loved one, we strongly encourage you to speak up. It may sound dramatic, but these are your final memories of someone very important to you. They could be indelible memories, so it's important that your concerns are appropriately addressed.

AWARENESS AT THE END OF LIFE

As the dying process progresses, your loved one may sleep more, waking only for brief periods. Eventually it may not be possible to rouse him or her at all. Nonetheless, you might still have important things to say. But can your loved one hear you? This is probably the most common question put to health care providers at this time.

Although no one can be sure, doctors generally believe that certain senses are preserved even in the final hours. Long after hunger and thirst have diminished, even after people no longer can speak or maintain eye contact, both hearing and touch remain intact. We've seen heart rates slow with a comforting touch, agitation resolve with the deliverance of sacraments or the voices of grandchildren. Nonetheless, family members sometimes feel silly talking to a loved one who can't respond. Some people may even try to wake their loved one. Instead, we recommend allowing your loved one to rest comfortably. Simply speak naturally. Now's the time to say the things you've always wanted to say. If the words don't come easily, try talking about family news, a favorite sports team, or even your day. You also can reassure your loved one that you and the family will be okay.

MEDICATIONS AT THE END OF LIFE

Although families frequently have strong opinions about medications in general, these concerns often are amplified in the last days of life. Is the medication enough to ensure that my loved one is comfortable? Should I ask the doctor to add more? Is the dose too high already? Is my loved one's confusion or sedation because of the medication? Are the drugs hastening his or her death? These are just some of the questions that may flash through your mind.

First, you should know that pain medications and sedatives administered responsibly by skilled providers rarely shorten the duration of life. If anything, decreasing the stress of untreated pain may actually lengthen life. Many patients in hospice care and their families believe that their doctor will be able to provide a lethal dose of medication when the time is right. We're all familiar with the debate about physician-assisted suicide. You may even have strong opinions about this controversial topic. For better or worse, hospices don't provide this service, and it remains illegal in every state but Oregon.

The desire to end one's life often comes from feeling very out of control over life and a failing body. Fortunately, physicians and other health care professionals can treat much of the physical and mental suffering that leads patients to seek a hastened death. If your loved one is requesting physician-assisted suicide, it's important to find out the reasons. This information may help the medical team provide better care, ultimately allowing your loved one to feel more in control.

Though many symptoms can be adequately treated, sedation and confusion are frequently inevitable in the final days of life. These symptoms usually result from the disease process itself, although they can be exaggerated and occasionally even caused by medications. Patients and families may face a trade-off: better symptom control with the side effect of increased sedation versus greater clarity with the potential for more pain and suffering. Be careful not to project your own feelings onto this difficult choice. If your loved one is capable of offering an opinion, ask. If not, try to look at the situation from your loved one's point of view. Carefully consider whether your loved one would rather err on the side of pain relief (with sedation) or clarity (with potential pain and suffering).

When giving a suffering patient medication, doctors usually begin at a low dose, then increase the amount gradually until the symptoms are under control. Even when medications are increased slowly and carefully, sedation and sleep can result. Is this okay? Providers are guided by the principle of double effect, which basically states that side effects like sedation are acceptable as long as the primary intent is to treat physical symptoms like pain or shortness of breath. Of course, medications can cause side effects in addition to sedation, such as constipation and nausea. For this reason, some patients may wish to defer medication for as long as possible. At the very end of life, however, these ill effects may not be as relevant. Constipation might not cause pain or nausea anymore, and mild sedation may even be desired. The benefits of pain relief and ease of breathing may seem stronger than the medication's drawbacks. It's truly an individual decision.

A SOFT LANDING

The goal of medical care in the last moments of life is to ensure that your loved one passes away as comfortably as possible. If your loved one is in the hospital or another inpatient facility, staff members typically will notify you and the family when they believe death is imminent. If your loved one is at home, his or her hospice nurse should provide this information. If you notice a change in your loved one's appearance or breathing and suspect that death is near, you may wish to ask a nurse or doctor about it. At this time, family and friends often gather to express their love and say their last good-byes.

After the death, there's no hurry. You may want to sit with your loved one for a little while, talk, or pray. It's okay to touch your loved one's body or hold his or her hand. If your loved one is in the hospital, inform a nurse that he or she has just passed away. If you're at home and your loved one is under hospice care, follow the instructions provided by the program. This usually involves calling the agency and requesting that a health care provider come to pronounce the death. If your loved one is at home but not under hospice care, contact the doctor and funeral home. We don't recommend calling 911, as paramedics will usually attempt to resuscitate the body. This can cause undue anguish to you and others present.

A last important issue involves being present at the moment of death. Many people feel an obligation to be there when their loved one takes his or her last breath. Unfortunately, this isn't always possible. Some family members and friends may live too far away to arrive quickly. Others don't find out until after the death has occurred. Real monetary issues also can stand in the way of being present. Unfortunately, many people wind up feeling horribly guilty when they don't make it in time.

Keep in mind that the exact time of death is almost impossible to predict, even for doctors. In their inspiring book *Final Gifts*, hospice nurses Maggie Callanan and Patricia Kelley (1997) convincingly argue that dying patients often experience what they call "nearing death awareness." Although not scientifically proven, this awareness seems to afford some patients the capacity to decide when they'll pass away. While some patients delay their last breath until surrounded by loved ones, others seem to wait until everyone has left the room. *Final Gifts* contains the story of one such person, Cathy, who waited to die until her parents, husband, and nurses all had stepped away. If your loved one died when you were away, keep in mind Callanan and Kelley's wise conclusion: "Cathy's final gift to the people she cared about was sparing them, and showing them her own strength in choosing to die alone" (1997, 207).

Whatever the circumstances of your loved one's death, be good to yourself. You've just lost someone you love very much. When you get a chance, take a look at chapter 12, which will give you some insight into the grief process. For now, know that whatever you're feeling, no matter how painful or unfamiliar, is probably normal. The situation may seem very unreal or far too real. Your grief may hit you immediately or gradually increase over time. Take as much comfort as you can in knowing that your loved one's struggle is over. But, most of all, rely on the people close to you and support them in return.

CHAPTER 7

How Should I Be Feeling?

Facing Your Feelings About Caring for and Losing a Loved One

Jason was fourteen when his father was diagnosed with liver cancer that would most likely be fatal. He and his father had always been close. For as long as Jason could remember, they spent every Saturday together, watching ball games, going fishing, or just playing cards. The day following his father's diagnosis was the first Saturday in years that they had spent apart. His father, who lived in a neighboring city, was very tired and decided not to leave the house. Over the phone, Jason told his dad that he loved him and understood the reason for his decision.

In the weeks that followed, however, Jason became increasingly quiet and distant. Even after his father regained some strength,

Jason didn't want to hang out like they used to. Jason's father became worried about his son. So, during an outpatient visit to the hospital, he asked his doctor if there was someone Jason could talk to. The physician asked the psychotherapist on staff to meet with Jason, who had accompanied his father to the appointment.

They met in a clinic exam room. The setting was particularly grim considering that it was the same room in which Jason's father had received chemotherapy only fifteen minutes earlier. The therapist began with a seemingly simple question: "How do you feel?" Jason sat quietly, staring at the floor. When the therapist shifted in his chair, Jason looked up for a moment.

"I don't know," he said.

"I don't blame you for that," the therapist replied quietly.

"Sad, I guess." Each word was slowly and painstakingly uttered as Jason's eyes continued to focus on a point about three inches in front of his feet.

The therapist nodded, took a deep breath, and an eternity seemed to pass.

"Is that normal?" Jason asked.

"To feel sad, you mean?"

"Uh-huh," Jason answered, hoarsely.

Wanting to understand a bit more about Jason's question, the therapist asked, "What do you think?"

"I don't know. It's like I'm being a wimp or something . . . Dad needs me to be strong."

Grasping at the meaning of "wimp," the therapist took a guess. "So you feel ashamed about being so sad?"

"Yeah, I guess."

"You know, that sounds pretty normal," the therapist said softly after a few moments.

Jason glanced up, appearing slightly relieved, then looked back down again.

The therapist filled the silence. "You know, I've felt that way too. Almost everybody has, even the strongest people. It takes a lot of strength to let yourself feel sad."

"Hmm," Jason murmured.

"When you find out a parent is sick, it's normal to feel all kinds of things. Sometimes people even feel mad or guilty."

"Mad?" Jason asked, glancing up.

The therapist nodded in response.

"And that's normal?"

"Yep. There's a lot to be mad about."

"Yeah," Jason said.

"Are you mad at your dad or at yourself?"

"Me mostly, for not being strong enough. Are you sure that's normal?"

"Yeah, pretty sure."

IS THAT NORMAL?

Most people have no idea what emotions are normal to experience when a loved one is dying. How could they? Most of us grew up in families where death was not talked about. Most parents explain "the birds and the bees" to their children but wouldn't touch "the cycle of life" with a ten-foot pole. Ours is a death-denying society, where the topic is at best ignored and at worst taboo. Jason didn't know what was normal because he was never taught.

If you're like most people, you've never spent a significant amount of time with someone who is dying. This is an odd fact considering that we are surrounded by death. There are six billion people alive today; this means that there will be at least six billion deaths within the next one hundred years. That's about sixty million deaths per year. Our purpose in bringing this up isn't to depress you, but to normalize your experience. If you're comfortable with your feelings about your loved one's illness, then you're better off than most. If, on the other hand, you're having trouble making sense of your emotions, your feelings sometimes seem out of control and other times almost nonexistent, or you're not even sure *how* to feel much of the time, then you're in good company.

There are a few problems with not knowing the facts about what emotions are normal during this difficult time. First, it leaves the door open for self-criticism. You may even start to believe that you're abnormal, bad, or shameful because of how you feel. Second, it can limit your ability to cope. And third, it can be hard to know if you really do have a problem that might require counseling. In this chapter, we'll cover all three of these difficulties, starting with the issue of self-criticism.

THE PROBLEM OF SELF-CRITICISM

Like Jason, you may feel sad, ashamed, or angry. Because Jason didn't know that these feelings were normal, he engaged in all kinds of self-critical thinking. "I shouldn't feel this way," "I'm being a wimp," and "I'm not being strong enough," are just some of the negative thoughts that people regularly experience.

Fortunately, many self-critical thoughts aren't completely accurate. Psychologists often refer to inaccurate, self-critical thinking as distorted. A major cause of distorted thinking when facing a loved one's illness has to do with feeling out of control. When nothing seems to be going right, it's natural to try to gain some control over what's happening. This may be especially true if you're a person who normally can deal with almost any problem. In their research, psychologists Thomas Shelley Duval, Paul Silvia, and Neal Lalwani (2001) have observed that the more people believe there is a way to solve a problem, the more they blame themselves for not finding the solution. In our experience, people may call themselves "stupid," "silly," "incompetent," or "wimpy." Unfortunately, when it comes to serious illness, there may be no solution that you can directly control. No matter how much you might want to cure your loved one, this isn't likely to be within your power. So it's easy to unfairly beat yourself up and wind up feeling more upset as a result.

Are you engaging in distorted, self-critical thinking? Below, we list some of the emotions that people normally experience when facing the illness of a loved one, along with the self-critical thoughts that often accompany each emotion. Read over the descriptions and see if you resonate with any of them. If you're thinking in self-critical ways, each description also contains information that might help you be kinder to yourself.

Anger

The majority of people facing the loss of a loved one report feelings of anger and frustration. If you feel angry, there may be lots of good reasons for it. People commonly experience anger because their loved one is leaving them, because they are frustrated by the immense time and effort involved in caregiving, or because they feel cheated that their loved one is no longer able to care for them in return.

People almost always criticize themselves for feeling angry. If you experience anger, you may find yourself thinking, "I'm selfish," "I'm only thinking of myself," or "I'm a terrible person for feeling this way." Not surprisingly, such thoughts lead to feelings of guilt and shame. To help you counteract these self-critical thoughts, we wish to be very clear: It's natural to feel angry when you're grieving the loss (or future loss) of someone you love. For decades, psychologists have known that anger, frustration, annoyance, and similar emotions are the brain's natural responses to being denied what it desperately wants (Dollard et al. 1939). And it's very normal to desperately want to keep your loved one alive, to have your own life back, and to be cared for.

Sadness

You don't need a book to tell you that sadness is a natural response to the serious illness of a loved one. In our experience, this sadness falls into two general categories. The first is altruistic sadness for your loved one. You feel this type of sadness because you want the best for your loved one and are distressed by his or her suffering. Although sadness is never a pleasant experience, altruistic sadness generally makes us feel good about ourselves. After all, we genuinely care about our loved ones. The second type of sadness involves feeling sad for yourself because you are losing someone special to you. Unfortunately, you may mistakenly view this sadness as being selfish, not being strong, or being a downer to your loved one. In our experience, however, patients almost always appreciate the opportunity to comfort their family and friends. Your loved one most likely won't feel burdened by your sadness. Additionally, your loved one may value the opportunity to talk with you about his or her feelings.

Empathy

Empathy involves experiencing the same emotions that your loved one experiences. When that person is sad, you feel sad; when that person is happy, you feel happy. Empathy can create touching moments of connectedness. But don't feel bad if you don't experience empathy very often (if at all). You're entitled to have your own emotions, whether or not they coincide with what your loved one is feeling. Remarkably, some people report that their sick loved one is in better spirits than they are. When such mismatches occur, people frequently believe that they should put on a happy face to avoid hurting their loved one. Almost always, such beliefs create more problems than they solve. Your loved one may be dying, but that doesn't mean he or she can't recognize a fake! Although it's important not to unduly burden your loved one with your emotions, don't be afraid to be genuine. If you're having a bad day, it's okay to admit it. Loving friendships and family bonds are based on authenticity. Why should this be any less true now?

Guilt

At some point, you probably will feel guilty about something that you did or didn't do. It's important to remember that guilt is simply a feeling; it doesn't necessarily reflect reality. Feeling guilty doesn't mean that anything really is your fault. In fact, it probably means that you are a good person! Have you ever met a truly bad person who had a conscience like yours? Guilt usually results from thinking that you should have done something differently. Psychiatrist Karen Horney (1950) first referred to this kind of thinking as "the tyranny of the shoulds." Nonetheless, we think that psychologist Albert Ellis's term, "shoulding on yourself," is a more apt description (Epstein 2001). If you're shoulding on yourself, try refocusing your attention on what you still *can* do for your loved one. Torturing yourself about what you might have done differently doesn't help anyone. It may be immensely beneficial to your loved one, however, for you to consider what you still can do to help.

Happiness

Experiencing moments of joy and laughter is normal and healthy, even when facing the death of a loved one. Positive emotions are a natural way for your brain to give itself a break. We often see visitors enter their loved one's hospital room with long faces, not because they feel as bad as their expressions would indicate, but because they don't want to be disrespectful. Our advice is almost always to allow yourself to feel whatever you genuinely feel. It's healthy to laugh if something is funny. We remember a woman who involuntarily laughed when her husband, who had lung cancer, bent his elbow and fluid shot out of his IV line like a squirt gun. Afterward, she criticized herself ruthlessly, saying, "I'm sick for laughing at a time like this!" It turns out that both her husband and his nurse also thought it was pretty funny.

Relief

Feelings of relief are also normal when a loved one is close to death. After all, death means the end of suffering. Moreover, it may mean the end of a long and difficult caregiving process. Because caregivers often make incredible sacrifices—giving up their free time, social lives, and even jobs—relief is an understandable response. For some people who may have experienced estrangement or abuse at the hands of their dying loved one, relief is likewise understandable. As with many emotions, however, relief can trigger intense self-criticism. You may find yourself having thoughts such as, "I'm selfish for feeling this way," or "Only a monster would feel relieved that someone is about to die!" If you're criticizing yourself for feeling relief, you should know that even dying people sometimes are relieved for their caregivers. One eighty-year-old woman with liver disease told us, "I don't want my daughter to know, because she wouldn't understand, but I can't wait for my time to come so she'll be free again." While the daughter was feeling guilty for anticipating getting her life back, her mother was looking forward to it on her behalf.

Numbness

In contrast to the intense emotions we've already covered, many people report feeling *milder* emotions than expected. If this occurs, you may wonder, "What's wrong with me?" or tell yourself, "I should feel sad!" Such numbness is normal, however, especially if it comes and goes periodically. In fact, many people report that it's a welcome break from painful emotions. Numbness only becomes a problem if you feel this way about most everything in your life (including things that you used to enjoy), or if it hardly ever goes away over a period of a few weeks. If this is the case for you, be sure to read "When to Consider Professional Help," later in the chapter.

COPING WITH NEGATIVE EMOTIONS

At some point in the process of losing a loved one, everyone experiences some of the emotions and self-critical thoughts just described. You're not abnormal, bad, or shameful for feeling the way you do. Even if you aren't thinking in distorted or self-critical ways, coping with strong emotions isn't easy. Your psychological strength is being pushed to its limits, and many of your most important emotional, physical, and social needs may be going unmet. At times like this, it's important to take good care of yourself. In this section, you'll take stock of your needs and make a self-care plan to help you cope.

Taking Stock of Yourself

Start by asking yourself, "How am I feeling?" If you are like many care-givers, you may ignore or muffle your feelings much of the time. When you observe your feelings, do you discover stress, frustration, sadness, or other negative emotions? Do you feel fatigued, run-down, or at the end of your rope?

Watching someone you love declining in health can cause significant emotional stress. Often overlooked, however, are two additional pitfalls of caregiving—physical and social stress. Physically, you may have to be awake in the middle of the night, sleep in a hospital room, bathe and feed your loved one, or help your loved one in and out of bed. You may feel utterly exhausted and even get sick yourself. Socially, caring for your loved one may mean that you can't spend much time with friends. This can strain relationships and sometimes create conflict.

Although the many stresses of caregiving probably can't be completely removed, they are signs that some of your important emotional, physical, and social needs aren't being met. The next exercise will help you identify which of your needs aren't being met.

EXERCISE
Knowing Your Needs

Take a few minutes to consider your needs. Open your notebook and write down anything that comes to mind when you read the following questions:

- What are my needs?

- Do I have unmet emotional needs? To talk about my feelings? To have some fun?

- Do I have unmet physical needs? To get some sleep? To eat better? To get some exercise?

■ Do I have unmet social needs? To spend time with family? To get out and have some fun with friends?

If you're like many people, you may be so busy caring for your loved one that you forget about your own needs. If so, use your feelings to tell you what you need. If you feel stressed-out or overwhelmed, your mind is underscoring your emotional needs. If you feel fatigued, exhausted, or sick, your body is alerting you to your physical needs. If you feel disconnected from friends, isolated, or lonely, these feelings highlight your social needs.

Don't be discouraged if you can't identify your needs at first. Keep paying attention to your feelings for a couple of days. Something will come up.

Taking Care of Yourself

It's important to admit to yourself that you deserve to be taken care of. Taking care of yourself will also benefit your loved one. This bit of wisdom comes from a very unlikely source—flight attendants. Should oxygen masks fall from the ceiling, airline passengers are told to put their own masks on first, then to assist children. Why? Because you can't possibly take care of another person if you become incapacitated. You can't continue to be there for your loved one if your own needs aren't at least partially met. Luckily, self-care doesn't require a lot of time, and it often pays big emotional dividends. The next exercise will help you identify things you can do to take care of yourself.

EXERCISE
Making a Self-Care Plan

First, take a look at the list of self-care activities below. This is only a partial list of ways to meet your emotional, physical, and social needs:

Things You Can Do to Meet Your Emotional Needs

- Listen to music.

- Do something creative: draw, sing, or write.

- Write in a journal.

- Go for a drive.

- Watch a movie.

- Attend a religious service.

- Pray or meditate.

- Talk to a friend about how you are feeling.

- Attend a support group.

Things You Can Do to Meet Your Physical Needs

- Take a walk.

- Get some exercise.

- Go out to eat.

- Cook your favorite meal.

- Take a nap.

- Ask a friend to help take care of your loved one.

- Hire a nurse or attendant to give you a break.

Things You Can Do to Meet Your Social Needs

- Have coffee with a friend.

- Call friends on the phone.

- Go shopping with an acquaintance.

- Go to a movie with a friend.

- Write a letter or e-mail.

- Talk about old times.

- Talk about your difficulties.

- Attend a support group.

Choose one or two of these activities that you would like to do in the next week (or add your own activities). Open your notebook to a fresh page and write "My Self-Care Plan" at the top. Then, write down your choices along with when you plan to do each of them. Try to do them as scheduled. After you've done an item, check it off and consider whether you'd like to schedule it again. If you don't complete one of them, it's okay; simply reschedule it for a more convenient time. It's a good idea to make a plan like this every week or two. Don't put this off. Caring for yourself will only take a couple of hours, and it will help replenish your strength, rebalance your emotions, and give you the energy to continue supporting your loved one.

The Burden of Self-Critical Thinking

Pay attention to your feelings when you consider taking time to care for yourself. Are you experiencing emotions like anticipation and contentment, or more like guilt and shame? If you're feeling guilt or shame for wanting to care for yourself, you may be engaging in self-critical thinking.

Many people criticize themselves for self-care. You may say to yourself, "I'm being selfish," "I'm not thinking of my loved one," or "If I really cared about my loved one, I wouldn't need time away." Such self-critical thoughts are almost always distorted. If you truly were selfish, unloving, or unconcerned about your loved one, you wouldn't be criticizing yourself in the first place. These thoughts simply prevent you from meeting your own important needs, with the result that caring for your loved one may seem like more of a burden than it needs to be. Try asking your loved one (if possible) or other people you trust for their opinions about your plan to take an hour or two to care for yourself. Do they think this makes you unloving, unconcerned, or selfish? If not, try asking for their support in encouraging you to put your self-care plan in motion.

Asking for and Accepting Help

One of the best ways to care for yourself involves enlisting the help of others. Although it may sometimes feel like you are alone, you probably are not. You most likely have a network of friends, family members, and health care providers that you can choose to call upon.

If you're already getting assistance from others, you know how useful this can be. If you're like many people, however, you hesitate to ask for help. Common thoughts about asking for help include, "I don't want to burden people," "Everyone is too busy," and, "Even if I asked, nobody would help." Our experience, however, is that most family members and friends are willing to help, at least a little.

The trick is to ask people for the kind of help they're able to provide. It may be that your cousin who lives in another state and has a busy work schedule can't easily be at your side. He may be a great listener, however, and welcome the opportunity to provide emotional support over the phone. Maybe your sister isn't a very good listener but can physically care for your loved one for a couple of hours while you take a break. Different friends and family members may help meet other emotional, physical, social, or even financial needs.

EXERCISE
Identifying Who Can Help

Open your notebook to a fresh page and draw a line down the middle from top to bottom, making two columns. In the left column, write the names of people who may be able to help. In the right column, write down the kind of help that each person may be able to provide. Make sure to consider people from all of the following groups:

- **Family:** Family members can provide a wide range of support, from practical to emotional, depending on the person and the nature of your relationship. They may be especially helpful when your sick loved one is also part of their immediate family circle.

- **Friends:** Like family members, friends can provide a wide range of support. Of course, friends may be especially helpful in meeting your social needs.

- **Coworkers:** Although family members and friends are generally better choices for helping with caregiving and your emotional needs, coworkers and even bosses often can be of great practical assistance when caregiving takes a toll on your work life.

- **Health care providers:** Nurses, social workers, physicians, and therapists are fantastic sources of help. Of course, it is their job to care for your loved one, but you may overlook the fact that many of them also consider it their job to care for you.

You've just made a directory of people who may be able to help with various tasks. In the coming weeks, use it as a resource whenever you need assistance.

WHEN TO CONSIDER PROFESSIONAL HELP

Supportive friends and family members can go a long way toward helping you meet your needs and cope with your feelings. Sometimes, however, professional help is necessary. In this chapter, we've emphasized that negative emotions, even intense ones, are generally normal responses to the serious illness of a loved one. However, we should mention four ways that negative feelings may get out of hand and require help.

First, negative emotions can last too long. Negative feelings are normal before and after the death of someone you love. Although you'll always miss your loved one, the intense emotions known as active grief usually are strongest shortly before the death and during the first few months after the loss (Chentsova-Dutton et al. 2002). As a general rule, if these feelings last longer than a year, you should consider seeking help. In contrast to these strong emotions, some people feel emotionally numb, even to positive feelings. Although temporary numbness can be normal, if this lasts past the first few months after the loss, you may wish to seek help.

Second, negative emotions can interfere with your daily functioning. Even while grieving, most people are able to complete daily tasks and keep up important relationships. If you find that your emotions are preventing you from engaging in needed activities or maintaining relationships with others, you should consider seeking help.

Third, normal guilt can sometimes turn into self-loathing or a sense of worthlessness. As we've already mentioned, most people experience mild guilt at some point during the process of losing a loved one. In and of itself, this isn't cause for alarm. Most people are able to recognize that this guilt doesn't make them bad or worthless at their core. If you begin to believe this about yourself, you should consider seeking help. Of course, if these or other negative emotions lead you to want to harm yourself in any way, it's important to seek help immediately.

Fourth, you may find yourself using alcohol or drugs to escape emotional pain. When used appropriately, alcohol isn't unhealthy. Having a beer or a glass of wine with a friend can be very pleasant. Alcohol becomes unhealthy if you feel that you need it to get by. If you use alcohol to sleep, dull unpleasant emotions, or cope with your stress or grief, you may have a drinking problem. This is especially the case if you're drinking more than a serving or two of alcohol a day, or if alcohol is interfering with your ability to work or complete daily tasks. Of course, drugs also can be dangerous to your physical and mental health. Illegal substances as well as misuse of prescription medications can cause long-term harm. If you fit any of these descriptions, think about talking to a physician or counselor about your drinking or substance use. If you have a problem, one of these professionals can point you in the right direction for help; if you don't have a problem, you haven't lost anything by checking it out.

Sources of Help

As mentioned previously, friends and relatives are often excellent sources of help and emotional support. Nonetheless, there may be several reasons to seek out counseling. First, you might prefer to talk with a neutral party, rather than a friend or family member who may be too emotionally involved. Second, for any number of reasons, you may feel that your friends and family aren't well suited to help you with your feelings. And third, you may have problems that respond best to professional support, like those described in the previous section. Emotional help for those with a dying loved one generally comes in two types: professional counseling and support groups.

PROFESSIONAL COUNSELING

As touched upon in chapter 2, psychologists, therapists, clinical social workers, and licensed counselors all can help you cope with your feelings. Such professionals aren't medical doctors but have special training in mental health issues. Psychiatrists are medical doctors that also provide services to people with emotional difficulties. Psychiatrists are less likely to engage in talk therapy than other professionals, however, and are used primarily when psychiatric medications are necessary.

Not all mental health professionals have expertise in grief or caregiver support. If your loved one is in the hospital or under hospice care, the staff of that organization should be able to recommend a mental health professional with expertise in this area. If not, contact a local hospital or hospice for a referral. If you contact a hospice organization, ask to speak with the bereavement coordinator; otherwise, ask for a social worker or chaplain. They should be able to recommend qualified mental health care providers. Or see the Resources section at the end of the book for a list of organizations that provide referrals.

As a last resort, you can find a counselor in the yellow pages. If you must resort to this method, however, make sure to ask the counselor if he or she has experience with grief or caregiver issues before making an appointment. In reality, you won't know if a counselor is right for you until you've met him or her. We recommend attending at least three sessions before concluding that a particular professional isn't right for you. Of course, if you're uncomfortable, you should feel free to discontinue therapy at any time.

SUPPORT GROUPS

Support groups, like counselors, come in several varieties. Some groups have facilitators who are trained in counseling; others, referred to as lay-led, are facilitated by nonprofessionals who have successfully coped with loss; and still others are leaderless, consisting only of individuals like yourself. Finding a support group that fits your needs can be tricky. See the Resources section at the end of the book for a list of organizations that offer referrals. The best referrals, however, often come by word of mouth. Try asking your loved one's health care providers. Additionally, it's often helpful to contact local churches or synagogues. Even if you don't belong to these religious organizations, they often are happy to provide recommendations on local support groups. They may even have groups that the general public is invited to attend. If you can't find an appropriate support group locally, there are now many online support groups. If you don't own a computer or don't know how to use the Internet, many libraries offer Internet access and a friendly librarian who can help.

A support group can be used along with professional counseling or on its own. The choice of whether to seek out a support group versus a professional counselor is largely a matter of personal preference. Whichever sounds most appealing to you is likely to be the most helpful. It's important to mention, however, that support groups are set up to address the most common caregiver and grief issues; they generally aren't equipped to deal with more complex mental health issues. If you feel that your difficulties are beyond the scope of a support group, you should consider working with a professional psychotherapist for a period of time.

IT'S NOT EASY

Facing the serious illness of a loved one isn't easy. You may feel confused or overwhelmed by your feelings and wonder how to cope. As you continue to read this book, we hope that you feel a little less alone in your experience. Although your feelings are painful, they are most likely normal. By recognizing your self-critical thinking, you'll be able to talk to yourself in kinder ways. And, by making a self-care plan, you'll be able to treat yourself in kinder ways.

CHAPTER 8

What Should I Be Saying?

Learning to Talk with Someone Who Is Dying

Martin was a charming man with a tremendous sense of humor. At age fifty-two, he had been in the construction business for many years and loved his work. A big kid at heart, he especially enjoyed demolishing whatever had been standing before construction. When asked about his work, a big grin would spread over his rosy face as he said, "Who wouldn't like getting paid to knock stuff over?" Unfortunately, Martin hadn't been able to work since he was diagnosed with a brain tumor six months ago. The tumor quickly took away his ability to walk, though his mind remained clear for quite some time. Because his wife, Jennifer, understandably found it difficult to care for him at home, they decided to enroll him in inpatient hospice, where he would spend his final days.

For the first month after Martin entered hospice, Jennifer visited him nearly every day. But as the tumor caused increasing memory difficulties and disorientation, she seemed to visit less and less. He was upset by this, constantly asking, "When is my Jenny coming to see me?" The hospice chaplain, Pastor Lauren Henderson, was saddened by the situation and asked Martin about it. He told the chaplain that Jennifer hadn't visited in nearly two weeks.

Chaplain Henderson knew, however, that Martin got confused easily. When corrected, he would often chuckle and say, "Am I talking crazy again? Soon I'll be saying I'm Jesus." For this reason, both the chaplain and Martin suspected that Jennifer actually had been visiting regularly even though he couldn't remember it. So, Chaplain Henderson decided to telephone Jennifer to reassure Martin that his wife had been there.

After three days of unsuccessful attempts to reach one another, they finally made contact. Much to the chaplain's surprise, she found out that Martin's memory was not playing tricks on him. Jennifer cried as she admitted that she hadn't visited in nearly a month.

After a few moments of silence, Jennifer added, "This must sound awful. I swear I keep meaning to come."

Not wanting to be punitive, Chaplain Henderson responded, "Well, I know from your husband that you love each other very much. My experience is that people have good reasons when things like this happen."

"I just can't bring myself to come," she sobbed.

"Because it's too painful . . ." the chaplain speculated.

"Yeah."

"It's understandably a very painful time. I can think of lots of things about it that would be painful, but what is the most painful part for you? I mean, the thing that's stopping you from coming?"

Jennifer thought about it for nearly a minute as her crying subsided. "I don't know what to say."

"To me?" Chaplain Henderson guessed, incorrectly.

"No, I mean to him."

I DON'T KNOW WHAT TO SAY

Like many family members and friends of terminally ill patients, Jennifer was at a painful loss for words. As her husband's health declined, Jennifer wasn't sure how to connect with him. His increasing confusion saddened and frightened her. Although she was afraid of confusing or insulting him by talking over his head, she was even more frightened of the possibility of silence between them. Most of all, she was petrified of how upset he might feel should the unavoidable topic of his illness arise. In this chapter, we'll explore how fear can stand in the way of talking with your loved one. Because many of the most common fears are based on distorted thinking, we'll cover information that may allow you to feel more comfortable. We'll also offer practical tips for sensitively talking to someone who is dying.

FEARS, CONCERNS, AND NEGATIVE THINKING

You probably share some of Jennifer's feelings. When spending time with your ailing loved one, lots of thoughts may cross your mind. You may think, "Maybe I'm making my loved one uncomfortable," "I hope I'm not saying something wrong," or simply "What should I be talking about?" Although these thoughts mean that you genuinely care about your loved one, they may inadvertently lead to feelings of distance, awkwardness, and dissatisfaction. As mentioned in chapter 7, problematic thoughts are often distorted. In other words, they may not accurately reflect reality. Below, we describe common distorted thoughts about communicating with a sick loved one. Each description also contains information to help calm your fears and allow you to better connect with your loved one.

I Will Upset My Loved One If I Talk About Illness or Death

People often avoid speaking with their sick loved one about illness or death. If this is the case for you, you may have compelling reasons for remaining silent. You may fear that such a conversation will cause your loved one intense emotional pain and possibly drive a wedge between the two of you. Unfortunately, the result of silence is too often just such a painful wedge.

We'll never forget Janine and her husband Gary, who was dying of lung cancer. Although they had supported one another for nearly fifty years, they never spoke about his illness. Janine told us that, at first, this silence gave them hope. "I thought if we stayed positive and didn't think about him getting worse, he might get better," she said. But after months of wordlessness, Janine felt terribly alone. She wanted to cry with her husband like she had so many times before and hear his comforting words. As these important needs remained unvoiced, every passing day amplified her grief. Although Janine didn't know it, her husband felt the same way, with one important difference—he had remained silent for Janine's benefit. It was a social worker who insisted that they talk about his illness. The conversation wasn't easy, of course. But from their standpoint, it was worth it. "I have my teammate back," Gary said as a tear streamed down his cheek.

In addition to bringing you closer to your loved one, a willingness to talk about terminal illness may help bring emotional comfort to both of you. Noted psychiatrist David Spiegel (1995), who has worked extensively with people suffering from severe cancer, has observed that speaking openly helps to "detoxify" death. In his book *Living Beyond Limits*, Dr. Spiegel relays the moving experiences of women with metastatic breast cancer who attended his support groups. These women supported one another through extremely difficult circumstances, even as some of the group members passed away. Although you might think that this experience would be disturbing to the women, Dr. Spiegel observed the exact opposite. Speaking frankly and openly about illness and death allows people to express feelings and talk about important issues, a process that can make death less scary in the long run.

Of course, every relationship is different, and speaking about death (or any difficult topic) may not be for everyone. Nonetheless, if you are suffering silently, consider speaking with your loved one. When such conversations are approached in a sensitive and caring way, the worst outcome usually is realizing that such a conversation simply is not possible. If your loved one doesn't wish to talk about it, allow him or her to change the subject. Most of the time, however, breaking the silence will be a positive experience for both of you.

I Will Upset the Family If I Talk About Illness or Death

Of course, families consist of more than you and your loved one. There may be anywhere from one to twenty other people complicating the decision to broach a difficult topic. Even if you and your loved one are comfortable talking about it, family members and friends may not be. You may fear that opposing their wishes will anger the family, causing more harm than good. If you decide to speak with your loved one about a sensitive topic, there may indeed be risk involved. In our experience, however, drastic consequences are a rarity. In most families, people can disagree and still love one another.

Although it's important to consider other peoples' opinions, it's your right to speak with your loved one. In most families, not all members speak with each other about everything. You may speak with your cousin about issues in your marriage, but not about work-related concerns. Conversely, your sister might be great at helping you with work problems but be uncomfortable discussing your love life. We aren't suggesting that you keep secrets; this can be a recipe for disaster. Rather, we're suggesting that, even in the closest families, deep conversations don't have to involve everyone, at least not at first. If you feel that it's time to speak with your loved one about a difficult topic, the conversation can begin with the two of you, then be extended to others when appropriate.

I Will Offend My Loved One If I Talk About Trivial Things

Much about loving relationships is trivial. No matter how deep your relationship with someone, the majority of your conversations undoubtedly involve superficial topics. You may talk about the weather, what you did during the day, the big game, or the latest gossip. Trivial conversation is enjoyable and, in many ways, forms the backbone of a good relationship.

When a loved one is very ill, however, you may find yourself wondering if such topics are still appropriate. Even if your loved one is a baseball fiend, thoughts like "I'm wasting his time by talking about the Twins" or "He probably doesn't care about stuff like that anymore" can prevent moments of joyful connectedness. Although some patients state that they no longer care about trivial things, many still do. We recommend asking your loved one what he or she would like to talk about. In our experience, there's no cure for the blues like a little chitchat with someone you love. Whether or not this is true in your relationship, asking what your loved one wants to talk about will point you in the right direction.

If I Don't Know What to Say, the Silence Will Be Awful

Silence can be uncomfortable. If you doubt this, next time you're having dinner with a friend ask to sit quietly for a few minutes. If you're like most people, you probably won't get very far. You'll be tempted to fill the silence. Although it can feel awkward or uncomfortable, it's important to keep in mind that silence is not bad. Some of the most meaningful moments occur in the gaps between words: a caring glance, an embrace, holding hands, crying together. Jennifer, the loving wife with whom we began this chapter, was terrified of silence. Realizing that she and Martin could no longer talk about the things they used to, she avoided visiting at all. At one point, she even asked, "What's the use? We don't talk much anyhow."

Silent moments take on poignant meaning to those who are dying. Words can seem less important than the mere presence of a loved one. In their research, psychologists Gayle Dakof and Shelly Taylor (1990) asked patients with cancer about the least and most helpful things that family members and friends had done for them. Notably, patients reported that their loved ones' mere presence was among the things they most appreciated. Moreover, when you're not sure what to say, giving yourself a few moments to think may help you find words that you're ultimately comfortable with. In fact, psychologist and end-of-life expert Dale Larson has called silence the "helper's friend." In his words, "if you give yourself permission to wait . . . before you respond, you will most likely be pleasantly surprised by the results" (1993, 166).

QUESTIONS TO GUIDE YOUR CONVERSATION

Even if no distorted thoughts are standing between you and your loved one, you simply may not know what to talk about. You may lament, "I wish we could talk more, but I don't know where to start!" In this section, you'll find general questions that may help you consider what to speak about with your loved one. Although you probably won't want to have conversations about all of these topics, see if any appeal to you. At the end of this section, you'll find lists that break down these larger questions into bite-size topics of conversation. You can even look over these lists with your loved one to find out what he or she might want to talk about.

How Are You Feeling?

For many seriously ill individuals, the feeling of isolation is almost as bad as the illness itself. We're not necessarily referring to physical isolation. A patient can have round-the-clock visitors and still feel emotionally isolated. Imagine what it would be like to find out that you have a life-threatening illness and witness your body weaken more and more. Dying people often wonder if family and friends could ever understand what they're going through. Having the courage to ask, "How are you feeling about all this . . . really?" will give your loved one the chance to express these feelings. Sharing fears, concerns, and regrets, as well as love and joy, can be a meaningful way to connect. Be prepared to listen.

Such conversations aren't easy. You may experience many difficult emotions yourself. Don't feel that you need to hide them or hold back tears. When you are genuine about your emotions, you give your loved one permission to do the same. Of course, this sort of conversation should never be forced. If this isn't a conversation your loved one is comfortable with, move on to something else.

How Can I Help?

Family members and friends often want to know how they can help a loved one with a serious illness. Of course, help comes in many varieties. As discussed in chapter 7, people have physical, emotional, and social needs. Caregivers sometimes focus so intently on one of these needs that they lose sight of the others. Maybe you've been concentrating primarily on your loved one's physical needs—preparing meals, hiring care attendants, or helping him or her get in and out of bed. Perhaps you've been largely addressing your loved one's emotional or social needs. Family and friends do all kinds of things to help, from sending flowers and calling on the phone to buying expensive health care equipment and traveling long distances to visit. Sometimes these efforts are exactly what are needed. Other times, you may not realize that there's something else your loved one really needs more. If in doubt, ask. You may find that something very easy for you to do brings great comfort to your loved one.

Is There Anything That We Need to Say to Each Other?

You may have unfinished business with your loved one: things left unsaid or undone in your relationship. Maybe there's something that you've been meaning to say to your loved one, something you've always wanted to do together, or a part of yourself that you'd like to share. Of course, unfinished business isn't always pleasant; it may concern unresolved conflict, estrangement, or resentment. It may contain echoes of things you wish you had said long ago.

Whether or not you decide to bring up these delicate matters can have real consequences for your relationship. The following principle may help you decide whether to discuss unfinished business: Ask yourself what you risk by *not* having such a conversation. Unfinished business may leave you feeling unsettled, especially when the issue goes back years. If this unsettled feeling is strong enough that it will prevent you from remembering your loved one fondly or lead to significant regret, then consider bringing it up. Use the following exercise to reflect on what unfinished business might exist in your relationship and how best to address it.

EXERCISE
Resolving Unfinished Business

It can be very difficult to decide how to resolve unfinished business. In fact, you may wonder whether you should try it in the first place. In your notebook, take a few minutes to list what might be unsaid or undone between you and your loved one. There may be no issues, several issues, or many.

Next, take a moment to consider what you might say or do to help resolve any of this unfinished business. Don't worry right now about whether or not you would actually do it. Just get your ideas out on paper. Leave some space below each possible solution you write down.

Now, ask yourself what would be the most likely consequences of trying these solutions. Write these consequences in the space below each solution. Try not to be overly positive or overly negative. Be as realistic as you can.

After you've written down the consequences, look back over your list and consider whether or not you would like to take action to resolve any unfinished business with your loved one. You might decide to address all of it or only part of it. On the other hand, you may decide that it's better not to get into these issues at all.

If you decide to take action, write down what you intend to do at the very bottom of the page. Consider acting on this plan.

What Do You Believe?

As the old saying goes, "Never talk about religion or politics in polite company." Nonetheless, for many people there is no topic more important than personal faith or spirituality. Although talking about this topic isn't for everyone, it can be very important for some people. If you decide to bring up the subject, be prepared for your loved one's convictions not to match your own. We've seen many dying patients get upset because of pressure from family members to change their spiritual beliefs or practices. Feel free to share your convictions with your loved one, but don't expect agreement. Your loved one will benefit most by concentrating on his or her own beliefs. If engaged in sensitively, a conversation about religion or spirituality can be immensely comforting for both of you.

Can You Tell Me About Your Life?

The possibility of death can make memories much more powerful. Decades ago, psychiatrist and geriatrician Robert Butler (1963) observed that elderly people engage in a normal and healthy process he called life review. Many seriously ill people cherish the opportunity to tell others about their lives. Recalling the events of their lives can give dying people a sense of closure and satisfaction with their experiences. Simply listening to these stories may be the greatest gift you can give. These stories also contain gifts for you. They're often enthralling, enlightening, and funny. If you listen hard enough, the wisdom they contain may even give you a new perspective on your own life. In chapter 11, we'll give specific advice on how to make the most of a life review conversation.

More Questions to Guide Your Conversation

Here are some additional questions to help guide your conversation on the topics discussed above:

How Are You Feeling?

- Are you in physical pain? How do you get through it?

- Are you feeling frightened about anything?

- Is anything frustrating you?

- Do you feel confused about anything that is happening to you?

- Do you ever feel like a burden on anyone?

- Do you ever feel alone?

How Can I Help?

- What are people doing that is helpful to you?

- What are people doing that is not helpful?

- Is there anything that you would like me to do differently?

- Would it be helpful if I _____?

Is There Anything That We Need to Say to Each Other?

- Is there anything you've been meaning to say to me?

- I've been meaning to tell you something . . .

- Is there anything that you want to do together with me?

- There's something I want to do together with you . . .

What Do You Believe?

- Do you think there's any meaning in what's happening to you?

- Are you a spiritual or religious person? What do you believe?

- If your loved one is religious: Would it be helpful to talk to your minister, priest, or rabbi about this?

Can You Tell Me About Your Life?

- Tell me about your childhood.

- Tell me about your career.

- Tell me about the most important people in your life.

- What is one of your favorite things that ever happened to you?

- What are the best decisions you've made?

- What are the most important things you've learned in life?

FINDING THE WORDS

Even once you've decided what to talk about with your loved one, it can be hard to find the right words. In truth, there is no one right way to express yourself. Our advice is to speak from the heart. If you genuinely care, the particular words probably won't matter to your loved one. You, on the other hand, may be your words' worst critic. We recall a middle-aged man who tried repeatedly to tell his dying father that he loved him, only to change the subject to football before getting the words out. Whenever the moment to speak arrived, he would think, "It sounds so sappy!" In the remainder of this chapter, we'll offer suggestions that may help you find words that feel comfortable.

Say What Needs to Be Said

In some relationships, there's so much to say that it's difficult to know where to begin. You may find yourself thinking, "There's too much to talk about. I'm better off not even trying" or "If I talked about all of this, it would just burden my loved one." And indeed, people with serious illness often are fatigued and have difficulty engaging in long conversations. Perhaps your loved one is confused and, like Martin from the beginning of this chapter, is no longer able to have complex conversations. There are good reasons why practicality should limit the scope of conversation. If possible, however, try to prevent these concerns from stopping heart-to-heart conversation altogether.

Ask yourself, "What do I most need to say?" Here's an illustration: Tanya was forty-two when her father was diagnosed with pancreatic cancer and given only a few months to live. They had been estranged for over a decade after he married a woman she despised. Sitting at his bedside, Tanya was filled with an uncomfortable mixture of guilt, anger, sadness, joy, and love. She wanted to tell him about these feelings but feared that it would be too much for him to handle. As a result, she decided not to say anything. Unfortunately, by the time she was ready to speak, her father was too fatigued to talk for long. So she decided on what she most needed to say: She told her father how much she loved him and asked for his love in return. Although the conversation was brief, it allowed them to say good-bye. It may be that you aren't able to say everything on your mind, but you often can say what most needs to be said. Use the following exercise to consider what this might be.

EXERCISE
Deciding What Most Needs to Be Said

Take some time to determine what most needs to be said. First, open your notebook and write down some of the things you wish you could speak with your ailing loved one about. These issues can range from completely trivial to extremely important. Don't censor or criticize your ideas; just get as many down on paper as possible.

Second, examine the list of issues you've written down. Think about what these issues might have in common. Look for a theme that several of them share. For instance, they could all be concerned with love, trust, money, hope, or guilt. This common theme may give you an idea of what most needs to be talked about. It might take a while to come up with this common thread. Give yourself a couple of days if necessary. When you're ready, write the theme down and reflect on how you might speak about it with your loved one.

Stay as Open as Possible

Perhaps the hardest aspect of any important conversation is opening yourself to the possibility of disappointment. In telling her father how much she loved him, Tanya faced the possibility that he might not return that love. Unfortunately, vulnerability can't be avoided in heart-to-heart conversations; in fact, it's what they're all about! It's important to be prepared for a response other than what you expect or need. When you speak to your loved one, think about what you need to say, not what you need to hear. C. R. Snyder (1994), a psychologist who dedicated his career to studying what makes people's lives most hopeful and satisfying, observed that a recipe for disappointment is having goals for other people. Try as you might, you can't control what anyone else says or does. You can only control what you say and do. Expressing yourself to another person is valuable whether or not the person responds as you had hoped.

Don't Shut Down the Conversation

Another aspect of openness involves not shutting down important conversations. Unwittingly, you may be saying or doing things that are preventing heart-to-heart communication. We remember Robert, an elderly man with advanced heart disease, who repeatedly tried to share his hopes and dreams for his son's future. Whenever he would begin the conversation, his son would respond by saying, "Dad, think positive! You're going to be around for a long time." Although his son truly believed that these words were comforting, his well-meaning statement shut down what might have been a cherished conversation. When psychologists Gayle Dakof and Shelly Taylor (1990) interviewed cancer patients, they noted that many of these patients complained that family members minimized the seriousness of their disease or forced cheerful conversations upon them. In contrast, patients found it incredibly helpful when family members calmly accepted the illness and its consequences.

When emotional topics arise, your first instinct may be to minimize or prevent strong feelings. In everyday life, it's generally not acceptable to cry or to say how we really feel. Everyone knows that the appropriate response when someone asks "How are you?" is "Fine." If we were to open up and say how we really felt, the other person would likely respond with "Look on the bright side" or "Feel better soon!" Such words stop further conversation by sending the subtle message "This is uncomfortable for me and I really don't want to talk about it." This isn't usually done with bad intentions. Emotional conversations are uncomfortable, and we just don't know how to respond.

Below, we've listed some common ways that people shut down conversations, along with alternatives that may help open communication back up.

Words That Shut Down Conversation	Words That Open up Conversation
■ Don't talk like that.	■ This must be hard for you.
■ Everything is going to be fine.	■ I feel scared, too.
■ Think positive.	■ Nobody can stay positive all the time. What's on your mind?
■ Keep fighting!	■ What do you want to do? I'll respect whatever your wishes are.
■ Don't get upset.	■ I can tell this is upsetting.
■ I'm not going to talk about this with you.	■ I feel stressed right now, but this is important. Can I take a break and talk about it a little later?
■ Be strong.	■ I'm here for you no matter what.

As noted, serious conversations are difficult. Don't be discouraged if you're unsure of what to say. It's okay simply to say, "I'm not sure what to say right now, but I really want to be here for you."

SPEAKING IN THE LAST HOURS OF LIFE

Of course, all the words in the world can't stop the inevitable. Eventually, most people lose the ability to speak as they near death. As discussed in chapter 6, although science can't tell us for sure, many physicians believe that hearing is often one of the last abilities to go. There are cases in which patients have awakened from a coma and recounted conversations that took place around them. For this reason, we always encourage family members and friends to continue speaking to their sick loved ones. If there are things left unsaid, this is your opportunity to say them. If not, talk about what is going on in the family, about your day, or even about your loved one's favorite sports team. Reassure your loved one (and yourself) that, although it will be difficult, you'll ultimately be okay when he or she passes away.

Some people are afraid to speak and not hear a response. This initially was the case for Jennifer, with whom we began this chapter. As Martin's brain tumor progressed, he became increasingly fatigued and preferred not to talk. Eventually, he lost the ability to speak altogether. With the chaplain's help, Jennifer became more and more comfortable just being with her husband. During the last few days of Martin's life, Jennifer sat at his side, her hand placed gently in his. She whispered that she loved him and that it was okay for him to go. She felt confident that he heard her.

CHAPTER 9

What Should I Be Doing? Part I

Attending to Practical Matters

When Christine's seventy-two-year-old mother was diagnosed with pancreatic cancer, neither of them were prepared for how quickly the disease would progress. Within weeks her health was so poor that she could no longer live on her own. Christine and her husband cleared out the den and moved her mother into their home. Shortly afterward the doctor told Christine that because her mother's health was declining so quickly, home hospice was the best option. Within a few days, hospice workers began visiting Christine's home. Of the many visitors, Christine was most thankful for the social worker.

On her first home visit, the social worker asked a seemingly simple question: "Are you your mom's health care proxy?"

"Her what?" Christine asked.

"Her health care proxy. It's another way of saying her power of attorney for health care," the social worker replied.

"I don't know. I'm not sure what that is," Christine said, feeling a bit stupid.

"That's okay," the social worker said, reassuringly. "A lot of people don't know. A health care proxy is someone who is legally appointed to make medical decisions for someone else."

Christine's mother was never the type to plan ahead. As it turned out, not only had she not appointed a proxy, she had never created a living will or even a traditional will. As if these issues weren't enough to deal with, Christine also knew that she soon would need to make funeral arrangements, not to mention eventually clean out her mother's messy home. And all of this on top of the fact that Christine seemed to constantly be crying.

As Christine listened to the social worker explain what needed to be done, she felt increasingly helpless. "Damn it!" she blurted out. "I don't even know where to start."

The social worker stopped talking, reached out her hand, and gently patted Christine's shoulder. "It's all right. Nobody does. I promise you'll be able to do this. I'll tell you what, we'll just take it one step at a time."

WHERE TO BEGIN

Health is fragile. It can change quickly and with little warning. Unfortunately, paperwork and legal affairs can't always keep up. That's why lawyers and health care professionals frequently advise anyone over eighteen to have certain practical and legal matters dealt with in case a health crisis arises. The reality is that many people don't. As a result, patients and families must navigate these complex issues while simultaneously facing the many medical and emotional difficulties that accompany the end of life. If you're in this situation, you may feel like Christine: helpless, confused, and unsure where to begin.

In this chapter, we'll cover three basic matters that you and your loved one need to address: advance directives, wills, and funeral arrangements. Although we can't possibly discuss all the issues that might be relevant to your loved one's particular situation, we'll follow the social worker's advice and take it one step at a time. For further information, most bookstores and libraries carry books that address these topics. For a general guide to the practical concerns of caring for an elderly loved one, we highly recommend *How to Care for Aging Parents*, by Virginia Morris (2004), which covers many of the issues discussed in this chapter in greater detail. In addition, see the Resources section at the end of the book for contact information for some helpful organizations.

ADVANCE DIRECTIVES

Advance directives are a way for your loved one to control his or her health care in advance. Specifically, these documents allow people to plan their medical care before they lose the capacity to make their own sound decisions. These matters can dramatically impact the unfolding of one's final days. Noted palliative care physician James Hallenbeck is fond of asking people to share their "fantasy death." Given that you will eventually die, how would you ideally choose to pass away? Most people say that they would prefer to die painlessly at home, surrounded by friends. Unfortunately, by some estimates roughly half of Americans die in hospitals (Teno 2001), often apart from family and friends and possibly undergoing unwanted medical procedures to keep them alive. When people haven't made their wishes known, the standard approach to medical care doesn't provide much flexibility. This is where advance directives come in.

Creating Advance Directives

Advance directives consist of two documents: a living will and a health care proxy. Because laws differ by location, you'll need to obtain state-specific versions of these forms. Fortunately, they're free and easy to obtain.

Many attorneys, health care agencies, and public libraries have copies available. You can also get copies from the National Hospice and Palliative Care Organization (see Resources).

Let's start with the living will. A living will is a document your loved one can use to make his or her wishes known regarding health care at the end of life. It decisively answers certain questions: What medical procedures would your loved one want to receive? What procedures would your loved one want to avoid? How does your loved one feel about life support? Would he or she rather be kept alive at all costs or receive care focused on comfort? Would he or she prefer to be hospitalized or try to remain at home, even if it meant forgoing certain medical treatments? These are sensitive questions, which is why it's so important to consider them in advance. What's more, at the end of life many people become increasingly confused or otherwise incapacitated. If your loved one is still capable of expressing his or her wishes, it's a good idea to complete a living will.

Your loved one should also name a health care proxy. Also known as a durable power of attorney for health care, this person will be able to make medical decisions should your loved one lose the ability to do so. Of course, it's important for your loved one to choose someone who is trustworthy, who understands the wishes set forth in the living will, and who is comfortable with the responsibility.

Honoring Advance Directives

Filling out forms isn't enough to ensure that your loved one's wishes are honored. It's important to complete two additional steps. First, distribute copies of the advance directive to any person or facility involved in your loved one's care, including doctors, social workers, clinics, hospitals, and nursing homes. Although you should keep the original in a secure yet easily accessible place, it's a good idea to display copies prominently. Too often, families complete advance directives only to have them accidentally overlooked by ambulance crews or other health care providers during an emergency. To avoid this, display the advanced directives on a wall or bulletin board close to your loved one's bed.

Second, your loved one and the health care proxy should have a heart-to-heart conversation about the end of life. Because living wills typically are written in very general terms, unforeseen situations often present unanticipated choices. In addition to knowing your loved one's medical wishes, it will help a great deal if the proxy is familiar with your loved one's personal values, spiritual beliefs, and hopes for the end of life. Such conversations aren't easy. Because the topic of death is painful, many people avoid talking about it altogether. Some people even fear that talking about death will make it happen. Of course, this isn't true. In fact, we believe that talking about death could save you and your loved one significant distress later.

The following exercise may be helpful in this regard. To avoid family conflict about medical decisions down the road, it also might be useful to include other people in this conversation. Chapter 2 includes tips on how to hold a family meeting about these and other delicate issues.

EXERCISE
Talking About Advance Directives

If you are the health care proxy, it's important for you and your loved one to have a more detailed conversation about end-of-life medical decisions. Below, you'll find some questions to help guide this conversation. We recommend sitting down with your loved one and working through these questions one by one. Feel free to add your own questions as well. During this conversation, keep your notebook handy so you can write down any conclusions that you and your loved one reach. These notes may offer indispensable guidance should you later face difficult decisions regarding your loved one's care.

- What are your feelings about your life? What do you most enjoy in your life? What is most meaningful about your life? What do you most fear in your life?

- What are your feelings about dying?

- What are your spiritual or religious beliefs about illness, medical treatment, and dying?

- What are your general beliefs about medical treatment?

- As people age, they often become less independent. What are your feelings about this?

- How do you feel about your current medical providers, care settings, and caregivers?

- In addition to me, would you like anyone else to be involved in making decisions about medical care for you if you're not able?

- Which is more important to you: being comfortable or living longer?

- What types of medical care do you want and not want?

- Do you have any personal hopes or goals that should influence medical decisions—for example, living to see the birth of a grandchild?

- If your heart stops beating, do you want the doctors to try to restart your heart (that is, resuscitate you)? Are there circumstances under which you wouldn't want this done?

- If you can't breathe by yourself, do you want to be transferred to the hospital and placed on a ventilator? Are there circumstances under which you wouldn't want this to occur? What if you would most likely never be able to breathe on your own again without a ventilator?

- If you can no longer eat or drink, do you want to receive artificial nutrition (tube feeding)? Are there circumstances under which you wouldn't want this to occur?

- If you were placed on a ventilator or were receiving artificial nutrition, is there a point at which you would want these interventions stopped? Why or why not? When?

- If you could choose, what would you like your death to be like?

- What do you most fear your death might be like?

- Do you have any other concerns or fears about the end of your life?

- Where would you want to be cared for while you are dying? At home? In a nursing home? In the hospital?

- What could I or others do to make you most comfortable while you are dying?

- Who would you like to care for you while you are dying?

LAST WILL AND TESTAMENT

A will is a legal document that allows your loved one to specify how property should be distributed after his or her death. Everyone knows what a will is for, but few people realize just how important it is. Virtually everyone should have a will, whether or not they have a lot of assets, as it can prevent heartache and save money in the long run.

Creating a Will

Your loved one will need a lawyer to ensure that his or her will is consistent with state law. For small estates, wills are often uncomplicated and attorney fees may be as low as a few hundred dollars. For larger or more complex estates, fees may reach the low thousands. In either case, it's usually well worth the investment. If no will exists, the court generally appoints someone to decide how to distribute your loved one's property. It's best to avoid this, however, because of the financial costs and family strain that often arise. Moreover, the result may not coincide with what family members believe their loved one would have wanted.

As part of a will, your loved one can appoint a trusted person to serve as an executor. This individual is responsible for making sure that property is distributed in accordance with the will. If no executor has been chosen, the court may appoint an attorney or bank representative to assume this role. An appointed executor will do in a pinch, but they cost more money and are often less efficient. If you or your loved one needs legal help with any aspect of a will, you can locate an attorney through the American Bar Association (see Resources).

Honoring a Will

After the death, the legal process of authorizing an executor to distribute property as specified in the will is known as probate. The probate process costs money and requires at least a few months to finalize. Although a minimal probate process is necessary even with a simple will, more complex wills require a more involved process. An attorney may be required to complete the abundance of exacting paperwork that's involved with more complex wills. Although court costs associated with probate generally are not excessive, lawyer fees can be high depending on the degree to which their services are necessary. Additionally, you should be aware that not all property is subject to a will. Trusts and jointly owned property, for instance, generally don't fall under the jurisdiction of probate court. A good lawyer can help you address what is and is not covered by a will.

Although the probate process is often burdensome, it's not nearly as troubling as the family conflicts that sometimes occur. When Amy and Ryan's mother passed away, they were shocked to find out that she left Ryan most of her assets. When Amy confronted her brother about this, he said that he felt entitled to the inheritance because it was what their mother wanted. Livid, Amy got a lawyer and unsuccessfully attempted to contest the will. Unfortunately, their court date was the last time these siblings ever spoke to one another. Although conflicts of this magnitude are rare, minor tension is relatively common.

In our experience, creative thinking before death can often help minimize family squabbles. We know one elderly man who, while revising his will, decided to ask his three children to each name one item from his house that they especially cherished. Although he decided how to divide up the rest of the estate on his own, his children knew in advance that they would receive these special items. Even if your loved one isn't comfortable allowing the family to play a role in drafting the will, simply explaining the reasoning behind a will can be helpful. If Ryan and Amy had understood why their mother decided not to divide her assets equally, perhaps their intense conflict could have been avoided. Because such a conversation never took place, they'll never know.

FUNERAL ARRANGEMENTS

Planning a funeral is no small task. For this reason, we recommend beginning as soon as possible—even before your loved one passes away. If you're like many people, it may feel wrong, awkward, or at least premature to plan a funeral before the death. In our experience, however, dying people often find great meaning and satisfaction in helping plan how they'll be honored. Knowing that the funeral was planned in part by your loved one may also make the event more meaningful for you. But don't push. If your loved one would rather let others take charge of this event, don't burden him or her with the responsibility.

The first step in planning a funeral is choosing a funeral home. There are likely several options in your community. In general, we recommend choosing a funeral home that is locally owned and operated. This maximizes the chance that you'll receive honest and personal service. Unfortunately, funeral directors have gotten a bad reputation. Stories abound in which greedy funeral directors sell unneeded services at inflated prices. The best way to avoid this is to do your homework. First, ask friends about their experiences with local funeral homes and their directors. Second, when you contact funeral directors, be sure to ask for a complete price list.

This will allow you to compare costs and services before committing to anything. Finally, you can contact the Funeral Consumers Alliance (see Resources) and inquire whether any complaints have been lodged against a particular funeral home. Their website also contains useful funeral planning information.

Once you've settled on a funeral home, the director will help you plan the details. Among other details, you'll be asked about what sort of casket or urn to choose, whether or not the body will be embalmed, how to transport the body, what flowers to display at the funeral, and what kind of announcements to send out. All of these services cost money and should be considered carefully. We urge you to remember that a good funeral isn't necessarily an expensive one.

If your loved one will be buried rather than cremated, you'll need to know if he or she has purchased a cemetery plot. If not, you'll also need to do this. Although the funeral director can help, ultimately the place of burial is completely up to the family. We recommend choosing a location that is comfortable and close to home. Because cemetery costs vary, you'll want to take financial considerations into account. Additionally, if your loved one is a U.S. veteran, he or she likely qualifies for burial in a national cemetery. You may wish to contact the Department of Veterans Affairs to find out more (see Resources). If your loved one has chosen cremation instead of burial, be sure to ask whether the funeral home can facilitate this service.

You'll also want to arrange a service. There generally are three kinds of services that take place after a death: viewings, funerals, and memorials. Viewings, which almost always are held at the funeral home, occur before the funeral and offer an opportunity for family and friends to see the body. This can be a valuable experience, as it helps people emotionally process the reality of the loss. Although viewings don't usually include formal speeches, funerals and memorial services often do. Funerals and memorials vary widely and can be arranged any way you and your loved one would like. Clergy or laypersons can lead these services, and friends and family members can speak, play music, or even show slides. Although it's generally easiest to hold these services in a church, synagogue, or funeral home or beside the grave, they can take place almost anywhere.

Most people don't know that there is a difference between a funeral and a memorial service. Because funerals take place before the burial, the casket is generally present. In contrast, memorial services can take place anywhere from days to months after the burial. The major advantage of a memorial service is that it allows people from out of town more time to arrive. Some families hold both kinds of services, often inviting different people. The family of one respected professor, for instance, decided to make the funeral an intimate family affair but to invite hundreds of his colleagues and students to a memorial service. Although a funeral director can help plan these events, you most likely will need to contact clergy and other participants separately. The following checklist may be helpful in planning both funeral and memorial services. For a small service, you may use only a few of these suggestions; for larger services, you may wish to be more elaborate.

- ☐ Select a date and place for the service.

- ☐ Make reservations for the location.

- ☐ Choose clergy or speakers and talk with them about what you would like them to do.

- ☐ Choose who will serve as ushers.

- ☐ If the service is a funeral, choose who will be pallbearers.

- ☐ Choose readings (Bible verses, poems, song lyrics, stories, and so on).

- ☐ Choose and send invitations.

- ☐ Purchase or rent any necessary equipment (microphone, stereo system, slide projector, and so on).

- ☐ Purchase a guest book, if desired.

- ☐ Create a program or handout, if desired.

☐   Select music, if desired.

☐   Order flowers, if desired.

☐   Purchase food or hors d'oeuvres for a reception afterward, if desired.

☐   For more elaborate events, consider hiring a caterer, event coordinator, or professional musicians if this fits your budget.

No matter what kind of services you plan, it's important to remember that a funeral is as much for you and your family as it is for the deceased. It's easy to get swept up in planning the perfect services only to miss the point of these events. They give you the opportunity to remember your loved one fondly, find support, and begin the grieving process.

PRIORITIZING: A MATTER FOR THE HEART

Having read this chapter, you may find yourself asking, "How am I supposed to do all of this *and* have time to spend with my dying loved one?" There's no simple answer to this question. We've outlined only three important issues that should be considered as your loved one approaches the end of life. Depending on the situation, there may be a host of other responsibilities—sorting through your loved one's possessions, contacting friends and relatives, and paying bills, to name a few. In the meantime, you'll want to spend as much quality time as possible with your loved one. Just as in any stage of life, matters at life's end require prioritizing.

If you feel spread thin, we generally recommend doing what absolutely needs to be done, but not necessarily more. This protects you and your loved one from legal mishaps while leaving both of you as much time as possible to spend together. You can usually find out what needs to be done from your loved one's attorney, accountant, or bank; a social worker from your loved one's health care agency also may be of help. Although it creates more work for you later, other tasks can often be left for after the death. If you're not careful, it's easy to spend all your time handling practical affairs and neglect important matters of the heart (or vice versa). Finding a balance between the two will help you minimize complications and make the most of the time you have left with your loved one.

CHAPTER 10

What Should I Be Doing?
Part II

Attending to Matters of the Heart

Don had been a professor since he was twenty-five. Practically a prodigy, he entered college at sixteen and graduated only three years later. As a sixty-two-year-old physicist, he prided himself on his scientific, logical approach to life. His motto, "Work hard, play hard, think harder," was the guiding theme of his existence. So when the doctor diagnosed him with a rare kidney cancer and gave him only a few months to live, he began thinking hard.

"I can cure this!" he said. "I've solved harder problems before."

First, he read what all the medical journals had to say about treating his disease. He combed through hundreds of articles. Much to his dismay, this reading made his poor prognosis even clearer. So he made himself an expert on the biochemistry of cancer. Hoping to develop enough expertise that he could invent a cure for his illness, he abandoned the medical literature and focused on basic research about how cancer cells function. After weeks of fruitless investigation, he finally abandoned this strategy as well.

By this time, his doctors were worried. Of course, many patients are understandably reluctant to accept news of having a fatal illness. They may initially question the physician's judgment or even get a second opinion. But Don was on the phone with multiple physicians every day, asking questions and challenging their grasp of medical science. He was very respectful, and many of the doctors even enjoyed the conversations. Nonetheless, it was becoming obvious that Don was in denial and couldn't solve this problem using his normal approach to life. He couldn't think himself out of this corner.

Dr. Reinhardt, his oncologist, was among those most concerned with Don's emotional well-being. Although Don was working hard to "solve" his cancer problem, he was missing opportunities to enjoy the time he had left. So during Don's next visit to the clinic, Dr. Reinhardt pulled his wife, Stacy, aside.

"I'm concerned that your husband is spending all of his time reading about his disease," he said.

"What do you mean?" Stacy asked.

"Well, is he spending any time with you and the family?"

"I guess not," she replied, biting her lower lip slightly.

"That's what I'm worried about," Dr. Reinhardt said, speaking a bit too forcefully. "I mean, he's obsessed with curing his cancer, even though we've tried everything. More than anybody, I wish there was something more we could do."

Taken aback, Stacy paused for a moment, considering what the doctor had said.

"So, what are you suggesting?" she asked, biting her lip harder.

"Try to pull him away from the computer and all the medical journals. I mean, get him to realize that his life is slipping away."

Feeling agitated, Stacy looked off into the distance for a good thirty seconds, attempting to gather her thoughts.

"Okay," she responded. "So let's say I get him to accept that he's dying. Then what?"

NOW WHAT?

Chances are you've asked yourself Stacy's question. Once you and your loved one accept that he or she is dying, what's left to do? Although this is potentially one of the most emotionally profound questions that can be asked, most patients and families only answer it in practical ways. They must choose what kind of medical care to pursue, whom to include in the will or appoint as health care proxy, what to write in the living will, and how to arrange the funeral. In fact, there are so many practical things to do that it's easy to miss the emotional tasks that characterize this important phase of life. Although they may seem less pressing, they too are essential.

In this chapter, we'll discuss five important tasks popularized by Dr. Ira Byock (1996, 2004), a celebrated physician and former president of the American Academy of Hospice and Palliative Medicine. Usually thought of as tasks for patients, they apply equally well to family and friends. Most health care professionals who work with the dying agree that these tasks can greatly help patients and their loved ones find satisfaction and peace. Nonetheless, it's important not to treat them as a to-do list. These tasks can't be rushed and shouldn't be forced on anyone who isn't ready. They need not be done in any particular order, though they often build on one another. Many people don't even complete all of them. What's most important is that you consider all of them, then choose those that feel right.

TASK 1: FORGIVING YOUR LOVED ONE

Even in the closest and most supportive families, people who love one another can harbor resentment, frustration, anger, and other negative feelings toward one another. Sometimes these feelings are relatively minor, stemming from statements people now regret having made. Other times, purposeful insults, heated disagreements, or physical or emotional abuse has created long-term rifts between people. If any of these situations have come between you and your loved one, it's important to realize that your feelings may be reasonable. Nevertheless, if you're reading this book, it's likely that you still very much love the person who hurt you. For this reason, the first task is forgiveness.

Forgiving the Unforgivable

Sometimes a transgression is so severe that it seems unforgivable. If this is true in your case, it's important to realize what forgiveness is not. True forgiveness is not forgetting, denying, or minimizing how much you've been hurt. It also is not the same as admitting that you were wrong and the other person was right. Instead, forgiveness involves breaking the psychological bonds that connect you with a painful past. It involves recognizing your pain and finding ways to move beyond it.

You may experience a negative gut reaction to the suggestion that you forgive someone who clearly wronged you. After all, you were the victim. Why is it your responsibility to forgive? The truth is, it's not. There is no rule that says you have to forgive anyone for anything. It's your choice and yours alone. Nobody can or should force you to forgive. Nonetheless, not forgiving is often harder on *you* than it is on the one who wronged you. Psychologists who study forgiveness find that people who display the inclination to forgive tend to feel less depressed, anxious, and angry than those who don't (Yamhure-Thompson et al. 2005). One research study even showed that people who were merely asked to imagine forgiving someone displayed significant decreases in blood pressure and muscle tension (Lawler et al. 2003). In many cases, people carry around resentment, anger, or even rage for many years. By forgiving others, they free themselves from lugging around this burdensome emotional baggage.

Most people think that forgiveness is something that happens between two people. Usually this involves one person apologizing and the other person accepting the apology. However, forgiveness can happen entirely within yourself, without your loved one ever knowing. Forgiveness is certainly easier when the one who has wronged you expresses remorse, but that isn't absolutely necessary.

Consider Susan, who was thirty-two when she found out that her father was dying of lung cancer. She had never been very close to him; he had left Susan and her mother when she was only eight years old. Although Susan had been harboring anger toward him for many years, this feeling turned to rage a few years ago when her father called her fiancé a "complete loser." Over the next year, Susan had hoped for an apology. When she finally confronted him about it, his response was characteristically blunt: "Oh, get off the cross Susan!" Five years ago, she severed all communication between them, sure that it would force him to apologize. In reality, he just stopped calling, and her anger and disappointment grew. But when she found out he had cancer, she was surprised to find that her feelings changed.

"He's a pompous, insensitive jerk," she told the chaplain at her father's hospital. "But I realize that I've given him way too much power over my life. He's filled me with rage since I was a little girl. He's dying and I can see he's never going to change. I admit that I love him. And if I'm going to have a relationship with him at all, I'm going to have to accept him for what he is."

For Susan, forgiveness ultimately wasn't about hearing an apology. Instead, it was about accepting him as he was—"a pompous, insensitive jerk"—while simultaneously admitting to herself that she loved him. She fully understood the pain that he had put her though, but realized she was suffering more by not forgiving him. Moreover, she never told her father that she had forgiven him. Instead, she decided to visit him in the hospital once a week—a commitment that she felt honored her desire to see him without rewarding him for his past behavior.

EXERCISE
Finding Forgiveness

If you're considering forgiving your loved one, it's important not to force the process. Take plenty of time to make sure that you truly wish to forgive.

Not forgiving is not a sign of weakness. To help you decide whether you want to forgive and what kind of relationship you'd like to have with your loved one, consider the following questions and issues. As you come up with answers, be sure to write them down in your notebook.

- Describe the way or ways that you feel your loved one has wronged you.

- Describe the feelings that you hold toward your loved one. It's important to consider both positive and negative feelings.

- Describe your loved one, taking into account both positive and negative characteristics.

- Look at the wrongdoing through your loved one's eyes. This doesn't mean excusing his or her behavior; it simply means being willing to consider why it occurred from a new standpoint. What was his or her life like at the time of the wrongdoing? What was your loved one's life like growing up? Does any of this help to make sense of what your loved one did?

- Consider what kind of relationship you're comfortable having with your loved one, given your answers to all of the above questions.

Now look over what you've written, making sure that your answers are honest and capture your true feelings. Did considering these questions change your feelings about your loved one or the situation? If not, this is fine. If so, revise what you've written to reflect your new feelings and thoughts. If you decide to forgive your loved one, consider how you would like to express this. It may be that, like Susan, you don't want to express your forgiveness directly and would instead prefer to approach your relationship in a new way. On the other hand, you may decide to say something to acknowledge that you've forgiven your loved one. Either way, you've done the hard work of contemplating forgiveness.

TASK 2: SEEKING FORGIVENESS FROM YOUR LOVED ONE

Many family members and friends of dying patients wind up feeling guilty for something they have or haven't done. If this is true for you, it's important to know that feeling guilty about something doesn't mean it's really your fault. Watching a loved one suffer with a serious illness is very stressful. As discussed in chapter 7, at times like this it's common for people to be way too hard on themselves. Nonetheless, there may be something that you really have done, either recently or in the past, that you'd like to apologize for. The second task reminds us that asking for forgiveness is often as important as giving it.

As with granting forgiveness, people often have misconceptions about asking for forgiveness. In our experience, the most damaging misconception is that apologizing makes a person weak or admits defeat. This belief often prevents people from putting painful conflicts behind them. Similarly, people sometimes believe that apologizing means admitting that they were the only one who did anything wrong. It may be that your loved one wronged you, too. Asking for forgiveness doesn't absolve your loved one of any wrongdoing. It simply demonstrates that you personally would like to have acted differently.

A final misconception about apologizing is that it magically will bring about a positive outcome. In our experience, most dying patients are touched by a loved one's genuine request for forgiveness. Apologies aren't always accepted, however, and even when they are, they don't always lead to complete resolution of the issue. Much like granting forgiveness, asking for forgiveness is a personal act. You should apologize because you feel that it's the right thing to do for yourself and for your loved one. If you're apologizing to bring about a particular positive outcome, you may be disappointed.

If you'd like to apologize, we suggest keeping it simple. The best apologies aren't lengthy or complex. They're genuine and from the heart, and they don't involve excuses. Often the words "I'm sorry" are more powerful than the most well-thought-out explanations. Once you speak these words, however, your actions take center stage. It's your responsibility to show, through your deeds, that your apology is heartfelt and that you're worthy of forgiveness. This doesn't mean being contrite or submissive, but it does mean not repeating your wrongdoing. It means being a better person as a result of your apology. Whether or not your loved one responds as you would like, asking for forgiveness and truly earning it helps you to grow.

TASK 3: FEELING AND EXPRESSING GRATITUDE

A third important task involves experiencing gratitude and expressing thanks. Each day we probably say "thank you" at least a dozen times. We say it when someone holds the door for us, serves us food in a restaurant, offers us a seat, or says gesundheit when we sneeze. For most of us, saying thank you is a social nicety; it's the polite thing to do. But only rarely do we actually pause in our busy days to count our blessings and feel thankful. Research by psychologists Robert Emmons and Michael McCullough (2003) suggests that we should. They found that when people counted their blessings on a daily basis, they experienced greater positive feelings as a result.

When was the last time you counted your blessings? Chances are you have a lot of things to be thankful for. However, it's all too easy to lose track of this when a loved one is seriously ill. As human beings, our minds gravitate toward the negative aspects of our lives, and thank heavens they do. If we didn't notice problems, we could never fix them. An unfortunate result of this tendency, however, is that we too readily overlook the wonderful things that surround us in each moment. Don't miss the opportunity to be thankful for what your loved one has meant to you and still does mean to you, and don't miss the opportunity to express these thanks. In our experience, one of the most powerful gifts you can give your dying loved one is your expression of gratitude. By saying thank you for the good things that your loved one has given you, you call attention to these valuable gifts. You help your loved one be aware of the ways in which his or her life has made the world a better place.

EXERCISE
Experiencing Gratitude

If you would like to experience gratitude and express thanks, try a task similar to what Emmons and McCullough asked their research participants to do. Every evening, take a few minutes to keep a gratitude journal. On a fresh page, write the date and the words "I am grateful for . . ." Then, write down aspects of your life that you genuinely appreciate, including aspects of your loved one. Keep in mind that nothing is too small to be thankful for. Even seemingly commonplace things can be powerful sources of gratitude; for example, "I noticed how beautiful the trees looked in my front yard."

After making this list for several evenings, consider whether you'd like to express your gratitude to your loved one. Although it's not necessary to say thank you for everything, a few particularly worthy items may stand out. Circle these and make yourself a promise to express your thanks in whatever way feels right.

TASK 4: SAYING I LOVE YOU

Love is undoubtedly one of the most powerful forces at the end of life. It is a core principle of most world religions and the foundation of close relationships. It deeply binds people together and makes life worth living. You wouldn't be reading this book if you didn't love someone very much. Unfortunately, people often take love for granted. When you've loved someone for years, it's easy to forget to say, "I love you," or show affection in other ways. If this is true for you and your loved one, try not to beat yourself up about it. It's a natural and understandable human tendency to get caught in the hustle and bustle of daily life and overlook what's really important to you. But serious illness often serves as a wake-up call, clarifying what truly matters.

We encourage you to think of love not only as a feeling, but also as an action. Many people have told us that they don't know what to do while visiting their ailing loved one. Speaking about his elderly father, one man said, "When I go to see him, he doesn't need anything. There's nothing for me to do, so I'd rather not burden him by visiting." But there was much he could do. He could love.

Sometimes love is awkward; sometime it's clumsy. It's normal to not know what to say. If you're comfortable saying, "I love you," this is a good start. If not, consider other ways of showing affection: bring your loved one a favorite movie to watch together, talk about a topic your loved one enjoys, buy him a new blanket, or wet her dry lips if she isn't able. Sometimes expressing love doesn't require any particular words or actions. When surveyed, most dying people indicate that they find the supportive presence of friends and family members beneficial, whether or not anything else is done (Dakof and Taylor 1990). This doesn't mean that you need to spend every waking moment with your loved one. It does mean that whatever moments you share present valuable opportunities to express love.

TASK 5: SAYING GOOD-BYE

Nobody wants to say good-bye to a loved one. Depending on your spiritual beliefs, you may believe that good-byes aren't forever. Nonetheless, saying good-bye acknowledges the reality that, in this life, your relationship is drawing to a close. Because the final good-bye will occur regardless of your actions, it's a different kind of task than those previously mentioned. This task isn't necessarily about actively doing anything. Instead, it involves gradually accepting and acknowledging the inevitable. It involves a process of grief that most likely will begin before your loved one passes away and that will continue for some time after.

People choose to say good-bye in many ways. We know one patient who organized a party to say good-bye to friends a few weeks before passing away. Another family decided to hold a cocktail party on the one-month anniversary of their loved one's death to celebrate his life. A traditional funeral also can be a meaningful way of giving closure to a life well lived.

Other people seek closure in personal ways. For Dorothy, saying good-bye to her eighty-five-year-old father was harder than she thought it would be. Over the last eight months, she had completed most of the previous four tasks. Although she had thanked her father for his love and support, asked his forgiveness for sometimes having been a rebellious daughter, and continuously expressed her love, nothing could have prepared her for the actual moment when he took his last breath. She immediately rang for the nurse, who called the doctor to acknowledge the death officially. As she sat at his bedside waiting for the doctor's arrival, she wasn't sure what to do. As it turns out, those fifteen minutes were among the most important in Dorothy's life. During that short time, she gently clasped her father's hand and quietly recited the short Irish blessing that he taught her as a girl:

> May the road rise up to meet you.
> May the wind always be at your back.
> May the sun shine warm upon your face,
> And rains fall soft upon your fields.
> And until we meet again,
> May God hold you in the palm of His hand.

WHY NOT START NOW?

Although typically reserved for the end of life, these five important tasks can be undertaken at any time. Almost without fail, patients and families wish they had discovered them earlier. As one patient joked, "I get cancer and now they tell me how to live!" Indeed, there's great benefit in living like you're dying. Why wait to heal relationships? Why wait to let go of pain and forgive? Why wait to count your blessings? Why wait to show how much you care? Some families fear that accepting the inevitability of their loved one's death will bring it about faster. Although this isn't true, acknowledging that all of us must eventually say good-bye may lead to a better, more satisfying life, and more satisfying relationships.

CHAPTER 11

What Is the Meaning of It All?

Considering the Spiritual Aspects of Dying

At age seventy-three, Elizabeth's health suddenly deteriorated. She fell several times, felt increasingly tired, and had frequent spells of confusion, intense nausea, and pain. Initially, she was pleased that her daughter, an emergency room nurse, took charge of her care. "We'll beat this," her daughter had said. They located a well-qualified physician who put Elizabeth through an enormous number of tests and attempted to treat her. Unfortunately, the first treatment didn't work. So the doctor tried another, then another, then another. Many months passed, and Elizabeth became increasingly weak. At times, she felt barely able to get out of bed.

Whenever Elizabeth experienced a new symptom, her daughter rushed her to the emergency room, where she underwent more tests. Every test seemed to find something else wrong. Her life had turned into a virtually endless march between home and the hospital. As Elizabeth began to realize that the treatments weren't working, she grew wearier and wearier of her medical care. Eventually, the doctor said that given her serious decline in health, she probably had only a few months left to live.

"He doesn't know what he's doing," her daughter said, annoyed. "We'll find another doctor who'll figure out what's going on."

That's when Elizabeth spoke up. "I don't want any more tests," she said. "I'm done trying to figure out what's going on!"

Her daughter was stunned. "I thought you wanted to fight this," she said.

Elizabeth gently took her daughter's hand. "Don't worry, I'm not giving up," she said. "But I'm sick of the hospital. You know, I've never been religious, but all this has to be happening for a reason. I just have to accept it, because there's got to be something I'm supposed to learn from it."

SEARCHING FOR MEANING

When a loved one falls ill, most people's first reaction is to seek a cure. In order to do this, they have to figure out what's causing the symptoms. "Why is my loved one sick?" they ask. They visit doctor after doctor for consultations, examinations, and tests. With every appointment, they repeat the question "Why is my loved one sick?" For the lucky ones, a cause is found, it's treated, and the patient gets better. In some cases, however, doctors may remain uncertain of the cause or treatments may not completely work, so the disease continues to worsen.

Eventually, the patient and their loved ones come to realize that the disease, whatever it is, isn't likely to go away. In our experience, patients frequently have an easier time accepting this reality than their loved ones. Family members and friends often keep asking the question "Why is my loved one sick?" even after it becomes clear that the never-ending treadmill of hospitalizations and tests won't lead to a cure.

In the story that began this chapter, Elizabeth had experienced a shift in meaning, while her daughter had not. Elizabeth continued asking the same essential question—"Why?"—but for her, it now meant something different. Whereas she initially wanted to know the biological cause of her illness, now she wanted to understand the *purpose* behind it. What was she supposed to learn from it? Was there a larger plan behind it? Making this shift doesn't mean giving up. If you and your loved one face this situation, you should know that it's possible to seek meaning and purpose while simultaneously attempting to cure the illness. Nonetheless, looking for meaning is an important step in acceptance. It allows you to see the reality in front of you clearly while also considering what deeper truths about life it may illuminate.

In this chapter, we'll discuss several ways that people find meaning when a loved one is seriously ill. Of course, we can't tell you what meaning exists in your particular situation or how you might best seek that meaning. Questions of meaning are personal and require extremely personal answers. Nonetheless, we hope that some of the ideas we offer will help you find these answers.

RELIGIOUS AND SECULAR MEANINGS

People often assume that meaning is a "religious thing." Indeed, every major faith deals with the meaning of illness and death. In Western religions, for instance, illness is often considered part of the divine plan, and death is God calling the sick home. These powerful ideas provide great comfort and understanding. Moreover, many churches and synagogues offer a supportive community that can assist you in your search for meaning. But you don't have to be religious to find meaning; the experience of caring for and losing a loved one can have a significant and lasting impact on your life no matter what your spiritual orientation. You may grow and change in ways you hadn't anticipated. Nevertheless, don't be discouraged if you don't find meaning right away. This doesn't mean you're flawed in some way. Just stay open to the possibility; it may show up when you least expect it.

PERSONAL GROWTH

One important way to find meaning is through personal growth. Psychologists Richard Tedeschi and Lawrence Calhoun (1996) have observed that, when faced with a crisis, most people experience some kind of growth. For instance, you may notice an improvement in your relationships with others, positive changes in the goals and activities you pursue, an increase in personal strength, an enriched sense of spirituality, or greater appreciation of life.

We aren't suggesting that you should be happy about what your loved one is going through. Illness and death are tragic realities. Nonetheless, they can reshape our lives in meaningful ways. Research shows, for instance, that people who report personal growth following tragedy often feel better emotionally (Davis, Nolen-Hoeksema, and Larson 1998) and have better physical health (Affleck et al. 1987). Misfortune also forces us to notice what is already good about our lives. Use the following exercise to consider how you might be growing, changing, or becoming more aware of the positive aspects of your life.

EXERCISE
Noticing Growth

Growth isn't something that can be forced. It happens naturally as we face life's ups and downs. Nonetheless, if you're not aware that growth is possible, you won't notice when it happens. In their research, Richard Tedeschi and Lawrence Calhoun (1996) have found that people grow in one or more of five distinct categories. These categories are listed below. Although not everyone experiences growth in challenging times, take a moment to consider whether you've grown in any of the following areas. At the top of a fresh page in your notebook, write "How I've Grown," then jot down any thoughts on this topic. Use this page in the coming weeks and months to keep track of how you continue to grow and change as you live through this difficult time.

- Relating to others: Have your relationships improved in any way? Have you met new friends or strengthened old relationships? Are your attitudes toward existing relationships different than before?

- New possibilities: Have any aspects of your daily life, however slight, changed for the better? Have you discovered new activities that you find meaningful? Have you made a positive change in your work life? Have you noticed new possibilities for your life, even if you haven't actually made any changes yet?

- Personal strength: Have you developed new inner strength or self-reliance? Have you learned new ways to cope with stress? Are you actually more capable of handling difficulties than you previously thought?

- Spiritual growth: Have you gained a new or deeper sense of spirituality? Have you strengthened your religious faith? Have you developed a new relationship with the divine?

- Appreciation of life: Have your priorities about what is important changed? Do you appreciate your life more than you used to? Do you find yourself counting your blessings?

PERFORMING RITUALS

Rituals are another important way that people find meaning when losing a loved one. Everyone is familiar with rituals. Perhaps you've performed them on holidays, in church, or even before ball games. You also may have performed rituals to acknowledge important life changes—graduation ceremonies, retirement parties, and funerals, for example.

The power of rituals lies in their symbolism. Think about the ritual of graduation. Walking across a stage and shaking someone's hand is no big deal. We walk all over the place and shake people's hands all the time. Graduation is special, however, because it symbolizes an important transition. When students step onto the stage, they exit one chapter of their lives, and as they cross to the opposite side, they enter a new chapter. Another symbolic ritual involves wine. Although drinking wine with dinner may be pleasant, it's somewhat commonplace. However, the same activity takes on powerful meaning during some religious services. The symbolism in these rituals fills us with emotion, gives us goose bumps, and punctuates the important events of our lives. Research shows that some rituals even facilitate the body's release of endorphins, which can help reduce anxiety and physical pain (Frecska and Kulcsar 1989).

Few people realize the power of creating their own rituals. Fortunately, one patient's father did. Donald was only thirty-eight when he was diagnosed with lung cancer. He was a professional photographer, making most of his living snapping photographs at weddings. On his days off, he loved taking photos in a nearby nature preserve. Although he never shared these pictures with anyone, taking them was one of his great loves. So, shortly after Donald was first hospitalized, his father decided to visit the nature preserve. He brought along an old 35mm camera and took photographs that he thought his son would enjoy. Donald loved them, and soon a ritual was established. Every time Donald entered the hospital, his father would visit the preserve and then show him the pictures. For Donald, this ritual was meaningful because it allowed him to share his great love of nature with his dad. For his father, it was meaningful because it kept a piece of his son alive and well. Eventually, Donald passed away. To this day, however, his father visits the preserve four times a year, once for every season. There, he speaks to his son, takes a few pictures, and doesn't show them to anyone.

EXERCISE
Creating a Ritual

Rituals are actions that symbolically connect you to something meaningful. They can be comforting, express feelings, bring about a sense of closure, or keep an important part of the past alive. They honor you and your loved one. If you would like to create a ritual, use the following questions to help you develop one that will be meaningful for you. Write down your answers in your notebook.

- What is the meaning of your ritual? Among virtually limitless meanings, rituals can be used to mark a life change, celebrate or commemorate an important memory, carry on an activity for another, and connect with living or deceased loved ones.

- Where will the ritual take place? Although churches, synagogues, and other sacred places are common settings, rituals can take place anywhere. Consider what settings will best connect you to the meaning of your ritual.

- Who will be present? Rituals can involve other people or may be performed alone. Consider whether having others present will enable you to connect more fully to the meaning of your ritual.

- What will be done? Reflect on what kinds of actions or activities will most connect you with the meaning of your ritual. These activities can require anywhere from seconds to hours, depending on what you feel works best.

- When will it take place? Although rituals frequently take place on important dates such as birthdays or anniversaries, they can happen whenever it feels right. Moreover, they can occur every year, several times a year, or only once. Consider what works best for you.

The key to an effective ritual is that it be meaningful for you. However, as you develop your own ritual it may be helpful to consider what has worked for other people. Here are a few suggestions:

- Lighting a candle in honor of your loved one.

- Listening to your loved one's favorite music.

- Looking through pictures of your loved one.

- Making a scrapbook for your loved one.

- Keeping an empty chair at the table because your loved one cannot be there.

- Writing to your loved one, then delivering the letter or keeping it.

- Donating money and time in your loved one's honor.

- Doing something your loved one would like, then sharing it with him or her.

- Writing a poem or story for your loved one.

- Creating artwork for your loved one.

- Meditating or praying about your loved one.

- Reading passages from the Bible or another holy book.

- Visiting your loved one's place of worship.

- Telling a story about your loved one to a friend or family member.

GIVING AND RECEIVING

Giving and receiving gifts can be an avenue to creating meaningful connection. In fact, many rituals even involve gifts. After Donald's father snapped photographs in the nature preserve, for instance, he gave them to his son. This gift was meaningful because it allowed Donald, who was confined to bed, to see his beloved park. Dying patients and their families often give gifts to one another.

Of course, gifts aren't always material possessions, as one patient realized. Ned always loved jokes. At age eighty-four, he had spent many decades collecting them. Whether you wanted a good clean laugh or a dirty snicker, Ned had a joke for you. He claimed that he knew over a thousand of them. "And not stupid ones either," he would add. "I forgot those long ago." When his heart began to fail, however, he grew afraid that his jokes would die with him. Consequently, over the next few months, he started writing them down. Unfortunately, just as he filled his first notebook, he became too weak to write. So he made an unusual request. He asked the staff of his nursing home if he could perform a stand-up comedy act. Happily, they agreed. His spirits rose substantially over the next day as he prepared his routine. Then, thirty-six hours later, the big moment arrived. Almost the entire staff and a number of patients gathered to hear Ned's routine. From his bed, which had been wheeled out into the dayroom, he delivered a stunning performance. His audience was in stitches. Although he died about a week later, he experienced the satisfaction of having given everyone the most meaningful gift he could imagine.

Though Ned might not have realized it, his audience also gave him a meaningful gift: their attention and laughter. Likewise, you may have the opportunity to give and receive gifts as your loved one's life draws to a close. Be on the lookout for these gifts and try to comprehend their meaning.

REVIEWING A LIFE

An often overlooked gift is your loved one's life story. Whether or not your loved one is a great entertainer like Ned, he or she may have knowledge, wisdom, and fascinating experiences to share. Unless these experiences are passed on, they may be lost forever. You are in the enviable position of hearing some of them. The great beauty of this gift is that it doesn't benefit only you. Your loved one also may find the act of sharing his or her life story deeply meaningful.

The psychiatrist and geriatrician Robert Butler (1963) observed that elderly people often share their life experiences with those who will listen. Through this natural process, often called life review, they can feel a sense of closure and satisfaction. Nevertheless, life review should never be forced. If your loved one doesn't wish to talk about the past, then the best strategy is to ask what he or she does want to talk about. On the other hand, if your loved one seems to enjoy sharing past experiences, consider using the following exercise to help make the most of this.

EXERCISE
Facilitating a Life Review Conversation

Reminiscing in a spontaneous way about the past is an enjoyable and meaningful part of many elders' lives. Research shows, however, that reminiscing in a slightly more structured way may be even more helpful, especially for raising the spirits of those who are depressed (Serrano et al. 2004). A structured life review is also a great way for your loved one's story to be recorded for posterity. Along with your loved one, take a look at the following list of questions. Consider selecting a few from each category (or adding your own) and setting aside thirty minutes to an hour for a life review conversation. Of course, if your loved one wishes to stop and rest, be sure to allow this. During this conversation, we suggest either tape-recording your loved one's answers or writing them in your notebook.

Childhood and Adolescence

- Where and when were you born? Is that also where you grew up?

- Describe the people in your family. What were they like?

- What were you like as a child?

- What elementary school did you attend?

- Do any memories of your childhood stand out?

- What were you like as a teenager?

- What middle school and high school did you attend? What kind of a student were you?

- Who were your friends? What were they like?

- Do any memories of your teenage years stand out?

Young Adulthood

- Did you go to college? Where? What was your major?

- What was your first job? What did you think of it?

- Where did you live as a young adult?

- Who were your friends as a young adult? What were they like?

- Do any memories of your young adult years stand out?

Adulthood

- When did you meet your spouse? How did you meet?

- What is (or was) your spouse like?

- Where did you live together?

- Do you have children? What are their names?

- Do any memories of when they were young stand out?

- What are you children like now? What are their lives like?

- What did you do in your work?

- How did you end up doing that kind of work?

- Did you like it? Why or why not?

Later Life

- When did you retire? How have you felt about retirement?

- What do you enjoy doing?

- Who are your friends? What are they like?

- What is the thing in your life that makes you proudest?

- Would you have done anything differently?

- Based on your life, do you have any advice for others?

- How would you like to be remembered?

WHEN AND HOW TO FIND HELP
WITH MATTERS OF MEANING

In other chapters, we've given clear recommendations about when and how to find help with medical, emotional, and practical matters. If you have questions about how to write a will, for instance, you should seek out an attorney. When it comes to meaning, however, matters aren't so clear. Because meaning is so personal and subjective, it's not always obvious when someone needs help finding it. Certainly if you believe that life has no meaning, especially if you also feel depressed or are considering hurting yourself, you should seek help right away. If you're asking questions like "Why me?" or "Why now?" or "What is the purpose of all this?" or questioning your spiritual beliefs, finding someone to help with these issues also may be useful. Nearly everyone has questions about life's meaning at one time or another. In general, if you feel that you would like help, it's probably not a bad idea to ask for it.

A variety of people can help you think through questions of meaning. As always, family members and friends may be immensely helpful. Because they, too, may be struggling with your loved one's illness or death, you may be able to explore these questions together. Additionally, members of the clergy can be very helpful. If you attend a place of worship, consider approaching your priest, minister, or rabbi. In addition, many clergy members are happy to help even if you're not a member of their congregation.

Alternatively, your ailing loved one's health care agency may employ a chaplain. As explained in chapter 2, chaplains typically are ordained ministers, priests, or rabbis who have chosen to work in health care. To be certified as chaplains, they must undergo rigorous training not only in their respective faith, but also in how to counsel patients and their families. If you would like to speak with a chaplain, ask the health care agency's staff whether a chaplain of your religious background is available. Even if someone of your faith isn't available, most chaplains are comfortable speaking with patients and family members of all religions without judging or attempting to convert them.

Finally, psychotherapists and support groups also can be useful when facing issues of meaning. See the Resources section at the end of this book if you need help locating a therapist or support group. If you decide to go this route, consider telling the therapist or group leader up front about your reasons for seeking help. This will help them to determine whether their services will meet your needs.

MEANING IN THE JOURNEY

We wish we had a crystal ball to tell us the meaning of life and death. Why do good people die? Why is life so unfair? Is there any purpose behind the many painful things that we all must endure? These are questions that every one of us must confront along the mysterious, sometimes frustrating, and often awe-inspiring journey of life. Of course, if we had such a crystal ball, it might take some of the awe and wonder out of this journey. As you face the serious illness of your loved one, we hope that the ideas in this chapter allow you to find a little meaning along the way.

CHAPTER 12

Will I Ever "Get Over" Losing My Loved One?

Discovering Life After Loss

Alison's father died of heart failure two weeks after his fifty-fourth birthday. She had always envisioned that he would be around until she was at least that age. She imagined that he would see her graduate from college, start her career, get married, and have her first child. But when his heart began to fail, this vision of the future slipped away. At first, he was only a little short of breath, slightly weaker than normal, and a bit sleepier. Over the next year and a half, he became increasingly disabled, needing longer and longer hospital stays. This continued until the family decided to bring him home under hospice care. Two months later, he peacefully passed away.

Thankfully, Alison's college was on summer break for two more weeks. She used this time as best she could. She helped her mother make arrangements for the funeral and entertained the many family members who came to pay their respects. She was surprised by how focused, calm, and collected she was. She cried immediately after the death and at the funeral, but otherwise felt numb. It was almost as if nothing had happened.

Returning to school was quite another matter. As she drove the eight hours to campus, she felt her stomach sink. In the coming weeks, her emotions were unpredictable. She fluctuated from laughing to crying, sad to angry, and angry to numb. She couldn't concentrate, kept forgetting to set the alarm so she could get to her morning class on time, and got her first ever D on a test. Her gut reaction to this emotional turmoil was to pick up the phone and call her dad. Tears welled up in her eyes when she realized he wouldn't be answering.

She didn't know how to live without him. The fact that he had always been there, on the other end of the line, meant that she could handle any difficulty. She was close to her mother too, but she had always been a daddy's girl. It was he who taught her to ride a bike, took her to the first day of kindergarten, helped her move to college, and comforted her when she had boy troubles. At just twenty years old, she made precious few important decisions without him. His death meant growing up and changing in ways that she didn't feel ready for.

She folded her hands and began to speak—not to God, but to her father. "If you can hear me, help me. I miss you. You were always there for me. I felt like I could accomplish anything because you believed in me. Now I've lost that. I know I'm twenty and should be grown up. But I'm not quite sure who I am without you."

THE GRIEF PROCESS

If you have recently lost someone you love, you may feel a little like Alison. In the weeks and months after a death, people feel an enormous mixture of emotions. It's important to know that practically any emotion you experience is normal—from expected feelings like sadness to more surprising feelings like anger, guilt, numbness, relief, and even happiness. You may also experience physical symptoms such as sleeplessness, muscle tension, and decreased energy. If you're like many people, you may fear that this roller coaster of feelings might never end. You may find yourself wondering whether you'll ever be the same again.

In this chapter, we'll discuss these feelings, collectively called grief. Unfortunately, in one chapter we can't possibly do justice to the complex experience of life after loss. In the Resources section, we've recommended a few excellent books on the topic. We also suggest visiting the library or a bookstore, where you'll find a number of other books that address grief in more detail. Additionally, we urge you to reread chapter 7; the feelings discussed there are equally relevant after your loved one dies.

LESSONS FROM THE STAGES OF GRIEF

You may have heard that grief occurs in stages. Elisabeth Kübler-Ross (1969), a psychiatrist and visionary expert on death and dying, observed that patients move through five stages as they come to terms with their terminal illnesses. Later, these stages—denial, anger, bargaining, depression, and acceptance—were applied to family members and friends, who seemed to undergo a similar process after the death of a loved one. But it turns out that grief is not so simple. People don't progress through these stages in a lockstep fashion. Instead, they move through them in as many unique ways as there are individuals. Consequently, you may go through the stages exactly as Dr. Kübler-Ross outlined, or you may skip one or more of them. You may race through them or drag your feet all the way to acceptance. You may even repeat stages. Even if the stages aren't exactly gospel, there are very important lessons that you can take from Dr. Kübler-Ross's work, no matter what your unique grief process is like.

Lesson 1: A Little Denial Is Natural

Asserting that denial is healthy may seem odd, given that psychologists have long considered denial inherently harmful. Research now tells us that this isn't the case. Ronnie Janoff-Bulman (1992), a psychologist and expert in psychological trauma, has observed that denial can be healthy in moderate amounts. It's the brain's way of "dosing" itself. Just as medicine is good for us, fully facing the reality that a loved one has died is ultimately good for us. But too much medicine too quickly can cause unpleasant side effects, and similarly, being forced to confront difficult grief-related emotions all at once can be terribly painful.

Dr. Janoff-Bulman isn't advocating ignoring reality. Instead, she believes that denial is the brain's way of making sure that we don't get too high a dose of grief before we're ready. In other words, the brain naturally gives us "denial breaks." These breaks allow us to relax, regroup, and ready ourselves for the difficult feelings we must inevitably face. So if you experience brief periods of denial, enjoy them.

Denial becomes unhealthy only when it's unshakable. In such cases, people sometimes fail to face their grief. Taking a temporary breather from your grief is healthy, but trying to avoid it altogether can have harmful consequences. As a general rule, the only way out of grief is through it. Below, you'll find a list of ways you can remember and grieve for your loved one. These activities may bring up a variety of emotions. If the emotions are there, don't run from them. But don't feel you have to face them all at once, either. Grieving appropriately means allowing yourself ample time to remember and feel the loss, as well as opportunities to distract yourself and regroup.

- Write a letter to your loved one.

- Write a poem dedicated to your loved one.

- Write about your loved one in your journal.

- Create a scrapbook of photos of your loved one.

- Tell stories about your loved one to friends and family.

- Simply speak his or her name.

- Say a prayer for your loved one.

- Light a candle in his or her memory.

- Place flowers on your loved one's grave.

- Visit his or her favorite place.

- Play your loved one's favorite song.

- Tell his or her favorite jokes.

- Cook one of your loved one's recipes.

- Give a charitable donation in memory of your loved one.

- Set up a scholarship fund in his or her memory.

- Plant a tree or flower for your loved one.

- Hold a gathering to celebrate your loved one's life.

Lesson 2: Grief Can Shake Your Faith

Faith doesn't just refer to religion. We have faith in lots of things: in ourselves, in others, and in the future. When someone dies, our faith in these things can be shaken. It may seem like the world will never be the same because your loved one is no longer in it. You may even wonder if *you* will ever be the same.

You may find yourself asking questions like "How could this have happened to such a good person?" or "How could the world be so unfair?" According to research by psychologist Melvin Lerner (1980), on some level most people believe in the old saying "What comes around goes around." We have faith that if we behave well, good things are supposed to happen to us. Many of us are taught this belief as children and don't entirely surrender it as we age. We work hard in our jobs because we believe that we'll rise in the ranks, make more money, or live happier. We're good to others partly because we believe people will be good to us in return.

But death challenges our beliefs. If the world is fair and your loved one has died, it's easy to believe that you must have done something wrong. As a result, people find themselves feeling guilty. Some people even try to bargain with God. They may promise to be more moral, just, understanding, or caring if only their loved one were returned to them. It's important to remember that your loved one had a disease with a medical cause—a cause that isn't your fault or anyone else's. Although it's natural to question the fairness of losing someone you love, ultimately death is neither fair nor unfair. It's simply an unfortunate reality.

In addition to questioning your faith in fairness, you may start to question your faith in yourself. Just like Alison, with whom we began the chapter, you might wonder "Who am I without my loved one?" This is especially likely if you and your loved one were close for many years. You may have trouble remembering who you were before that person came into your life. People often define themselves by the roles they play in close relationships. They think of themselves as spouses, siblings, children, friends, mentors, or caregivers. When someone dies, you may lose one or more of these important roles. In this situation, it's natural to feel upset, confused, sad, and even angry. Grief takes time because it entails accepting the loss of certain roles and redefining yourself.

During this time of changes, it's important to remind yourself of what hasn't changed. Although much has shifted, there are some constants in your life; your remaining friends and family are a good start. Take comfort in what is stable. Use this as a starting point from which to build new faith in who you are now that your loved one has departed.

Lesson 3: Grief Usually Leads to Acceptance

Central to Dr. Kübler-Ross's stages is the notion that grief is a process that eventually leads to acceptance. Although you'll always miss your loved one, the painful emotions you feel shortly after the death almost certainly will pass. It can be very comforting to keep this in mind. If you tell yourself, "This will never end," "I'm weak for feeling this way," "I'm going crazy," or other negative (and probably not fully accurate) statements, then you'll wind up feeling needlessly worse. If instead you reassure yourself with thoughts like "This is normal and won't last forever," then it will be easier to honor your loss without added burden.

Still, it's important not to rush grief. Well-meaning people will give you all kinds of estimates on how long the grief process lasts. One person may tell you a few weeks, while others might say anywhere from a few months to a number of years. These people aren't lying; they're simply telling you about *their* experiences. Grief is very personal, and you're entitled to your own schedule. While people sometimes continue to experience moments of sadness even several years after losing a loved one, most people's strong feelings of grief lessen substantially within a few months (Chentsova-Dutton et al. 2002). Don't criticize yourself, however, if your grief doesn't act like most people's. Grief isn't a race to the finish line. Accept your feelings as much as possible while simultaneously reminding yourself that they most likely will soften with time.

REGRET, GUILT, AND SELF-CRITICISM

For some people, emotions like regret and guilt are major aspects of grief. As discussed in chapter 7, these emotions are normal both before and after the death of a loved one. And although sometimes there really is something worth feeling guilty about, in our experience guilt often results from being much too hard on yourself. It's important to notice this distorted thinking if it occurs, because it can stand in the way of healthy grieving. In the next few sections, we describe a few common ways that bereaved individuals sometimes are way too hard on themselves.

I Didn't Say or Do Enough

People frequently regret having left something unsaid or undone in their relationship with their loved one. Perhaps you feel that you should have expressed more appreciation for your loved one or said "I love you" more often. You may feel that you should have been there for your loved one's death, should have visited more often, or should have taken him or her to a favorite spot one last time. As discussed in chapter 7, this kind of self-critical thinking is called "the tyranny of the shoulds."

Unfortunately, people often concentrate on what they didn't do and what they should have done, but forget about all they actually did. There may be many ways that your relationship with your loved one was strong. We remember Liz, the daughter of an elderly man who passed away from lung cancer. Throughout his ordeal, she flew across the country four times to be with him, leaving her own work and family behind. When she wasn't physically present, she called often to speak with her father and mother on the phone. To her dismay, when she heard of a sudden decline in his health, she flew to his bedside only to find that she missed his death. She tortured herself for weeks, accusing herself of being a bad daughter because she should have been there. Finally, her mother flew across the country to be with Liz. "Your father didn't care if you were there or not when he died," she said. "He knew you loved him; you showed him that over and over again." Just like Liz, it's important not to lose sight of what you actually were able to do for your loved one.

I Made the Wrong Decision

Some caregivers blame themselves for having made a wrong decision about their loved ones' medical care. For instance, Craig blamed himself for the circumstances of his grandmother's death. His eighty-five-year-old grandmother, Dee, had always said she wanted to die at home, where she had lived for over six decades. In recent months, he had moved into her home to care for her. Although Dee was increasingly confused and weak, she still seemed relatively healthy to him. Then Dee fell and fractured her hip. Over the phone, the doctor advised bringing her to the hospital by ambulance.

"We may be able to fix the hip," she said. "But we have to examine it first." The trip to the hospital was traumatic for Dee, who cried out in pain and confusion. Unsure of where she was, she repeatedly called for Craig but ultimately was inconsolable. Unfortunately, just hours after entering the hospital, she passed away. Craig felt horribly guilty. "I should have kept her home," Craig said. "It's all my fault she died away from home."

This is a difficult story. In retrospect, it probably would have been better for Dee to remain at home. With time, however, Craig came to realize that he wasn't at fault for how his grandmother passed away. He made the best decision he could with the information he had at the time. He didn't know she was going to die so quickly. All he knew was that his grandmother was in pain and the doctor recommended bringing her to the hospital. It wasn't his fault, it wasn't the doctor's fault, and it wasn't the hospital's fault. Dee simply was very ill.

Similarly, if you feel that you've made a wrong choice, ask yourself whether you made the best decision you could given the information you had *at the time*. No one is to blame for not seeing the future.

I'm a Terrible Person

As previously mentioned, lingering feelings of mild regret or guilt are common among bereaved people. Generally, these feelings are manageable and rarely cause long-term difficulties. Feelings of self-loathing are potentially more problematic. If you believe that your loved one's death is all your fault, you may begin to feel worthless and awful. Normal guilt comes from wishing you had done something differently. Normal guilt turns into self-loathing, however, when you believe you are terrible because of your actions. Just like regret and guilt, self-loathing often results from being way too hard on yourself. Unfortunately, it is difficult for people who feel this way to see this on their own. Consequently, for people experiencing these thoughts, we often recommend seeking out a grief counselor, support group, or psychotherapy. In the remainder of this chapter, we'll discuss how to find help when you need it.

WHEN AND HOW TO FIND HELP WITH GRIEF

When should you find help with grief? The answer is always. Finding people to support you is perhaps the most important thing you can do following the loss of someone you love. One research study found that, even two years after the loss, people with poor social support tended to have greater emotional distress than those with better social support (Vachon et al. 1982). This doesn't mean you have to spend every waking moment with people. Nonetheless, the time you spend with others may be valuable.

Friends and family members can support you in more ways than one. They can buoy you up emotionally, provide distraction and entertainment, and even help with the practical matters of day-to-day living. Most importantly, however, they can listen. It can be extraordinarily healing to share your grief. In a survey by psychologists Darrin Lehman, John Ellard, and Camille Wortman (1986), bereaved individuals said that the most helpful thing that friends and family members did during their grief process was simply to listen. Although you won't always feel like talking, it's comforting to know that someone is available when you need a sympathetic ear.

Of course, friends and family members are sometimes not enough. For many reasons, you may wish to seek out professional counseling or support groups. First, support groups are a great way to meet others who share the experience of loss. These groups, which are led either by professional therapists or experienced laypeople, are often a source of longtime friendships. Second, support groups and professional counselors are a great alternative when it seems inappropriate to rely exclusively on friends and family. Although friends and family members will often surprise you with their willingness to listen, sometimes an impartial ear simply seems more helpful. Finally, as mentioned in chapter 7, you should consider seeking professional support when negative emotions or grief either last for an extended period of time or interfere significantly with your life. If you feel this might be the case, be sure to reread the section of that chapter entitled "When to Consider Professional Help." See the Resources section for help finding bereavement support groups and professional counselors in your area.

LOOKING FORWARD: THE POSSIBILITY OF GROWTH

You've been through a struggle; take time to recover and grieve. The truth is that you will never stop missing your loved one, and you'll never be happy that he or she is gone. As you grieve, however, don't ignore ways that you might be growing or becoming stronger. Psychologists Christopher Davis, Susan Nolen-Hoeksema, and Judith Larson (1998) asked bereaved individuals about their lives approximately a year after the loss. Interestingly, 80 percent of people said that, along with the understandably negative feelings that accompany grief, they also found some benefit. People who experience loss sometimes grow closer to their family, become more spiritual, realize the importance of each new day, or gain a new philosophy on life.

So often, grief is about looking backward—on your loved one's life, your relationship, your struggle to be a caregiver, and, ultimately, the sad fact of death. It's important to look back; it honors your loved one's memory and your own feelings. You'll never stop remembering, nor should you. Nonetheless, through grieving, you'll slowly turn your sights forward, toward the future. As you grieve, allow plenty of time to experience your feelings, whatever they may be, take comfort in friends and family, and be as kind to yourself as possible. The future will be there, waiting.

Resources

RECOMMENDED BOOKS ON GRIEF AND LOSS

Kübler-Ross, Elisabeth, and David Kessler. 2005. *On Grief and Grieving: Finding the Meaning of Grief Through the Five Stages of Loss.* New York: Scribner.

Levinson, Deborah S. 2004. *Surviving the Death of Your Spouse.* Oakland, CA: New Harbinger Publications.

Noel, Brook, and Pamela D. Blair. 2000. *I Wasn't Ready to Say Goodbye: Surviving, Coping, and Healing After the Death of a Loved One.* Milwaukee, WI: Champion Press.

Rando, Therese A. 1988. *How to Go On Living When Someone You Love Dies.* Lexington, MA: Lexington Books.

RESOURCES FOR FINDING PROFESSIONAL GRIEF COUNSELING

American Association for Marriage and Family Therapy: 703-838-9808; www.therapistlocator.net.

American Psychological Association: 800-964-2000; www.apahelpcenter .org.

National Association of Social Workers: 800-638-8799; www.socialworkers .org.

RESOURCES FOR FINDING GRIEF AND CAREGIVER SUPPORT GROUPS

AARP Grief and Loss Resources: 888-687-2277; www.aarp.org/families/ grief_loss.

Alzheimer's Association: 800-272-3900; www.alz.org.

American Cancer Society: 800-227-2345; www.cancer.org.

The Compassionate Friends (for families who have lost a child): 800-638-8799; www.compassionatefriends.net.

Department of Health and Human Services Eldercare Locator: 800-677-1116; www.eldercare.gov.

National Health Information Center Healthfinder: www.healthfinder.gov.

National Hospice and Palliative Care Organization: 800-658-8898; www .nhpco.org.

RESOURCES FOR FINDING ONLINE GRIEF SUPPORT GROUPS

AARP message boards: www.aarp.org/boards.

American Cancer Society: www.cancer.org.

GriefNet: www.griefnet.org.

Grief Recovery Online for All Bereaved (GROWW): www.groww.org.

Helpguide: www.helpguide.org.

SeniorNet: www.seniornet.org.

RESOURCES FOR HELP WITH PRACTICAL MATTERS

Help with Advance Directives

AARP End of Life Resources: 888-687-2277; www.aarp.org/families/end_life. *Provides excellent information on advanced directives and many other topics.*

American Bar Association Commission on Law and Aging: 800-285-2221; www.abanet.org/aging/toolkit. *Provides useful information and instructions on preparing advance directives.*

National Hospice and Palliative Care Organization: 800-658-8898; www.nhpco.org. *Provides advanced directive forms for all fifty states.*

Help with Wills

AARP End of Life Resources: 888-687-2277; www.aarp.org/families/end_life. *Provides excellent information on wills and many other topics.*

American Bar Association Consumers' Guide to Legal Help: 800-285-2221; www.findlegalhelp.org. *Provides resources for finding a local attorney.*

Help with Funerals

AARP Grief and Loss Resources: 888-687-2277; www.aarp.com/families/grief_loss. *Provides general information on funeral arrangements and many other topics.*

Department of Veterans Affairs: 800-827-1000; www.cem.va.gov. *Offers information on burial benefits and burial in a national cemetery.*

Funeral Consumers Alliance: 800-765-0107; www.funerals.org. *Posts consumer alerts regarding funeral homes.*

National Funeral Directors Association: 800-228-6332; www.nfda.org/consumerresources. *Offers useful information for planning a funeral as well as a service for finding local funeral homes.*

HELP FINDING OTHER ONLINE RESOURCES

Growth House: www.growthhouse.org. *This excellent website serves as a clearinghouse for information about most aspects of end-of-life planning and care.*

References

Affleck, G., H. Tennen, S. Croog, and S. Levine. 1987. Causal attribution, perceived benefits, and morbidity after a heart attack: An 8-year study. *Journal of Consulting and Clinical Psychology* 55(1):29-35.

Beresford, L. 1993. *The Hospice Handbook: A Complete Guide.* New York: Little, Brown & Company.

Bortz, W. M. 2001. *Living Longer for Dummies.* New York: Hungry Minds.

Butler, R. N. 1963. The life review: An interpretation of reminiscence in the aged. *Psychiatry* 26:65-76.

Byock, I. 1996. The nature of suffering and the nature of opportunity at the end of life. *Clinics in Geriatric Medicine* 12(2):237-252.

Byock, I. 2004. *The Four Things That Matter Most: A Book About Living.* New York: Free Press.

Callanan, M., and P. Kelley. 1997. *Final Gifts*. New York: Bantam.

Chentsova-Dutton, Y., S. Shucter, S. Hutchin, L. Strause, K. Burns, L. Dunn, M. Miller, and S. Zisook. 2002. Depression and grief reactions in hospice caregivers: From pre-death to 1 year afterwards. *Journal of Affective Disorders* 69(1):53-60.

Connor, S. R., B. Pyenson, K. Fitch, C. Spence, and K. Iwasaki. 2007. Comparing hospice and nonhospice patient survival among patients who die within a three-year window. *Journal of Pain and Symptom Management* 33(3):238-246.

Dakof, G. A., and S. E. Taylor. 1990. Victims' perceptions of social support: What is helpful from whom? *Journal of Personality and Social Psychology* 58(1):80-89.

Davis, C. G., S. Nolen-Hoeksema, and J. Larson. 1998. Making sense of loss and benefiting from the experience: Two construals of meaning. *Journal of Personality and Social Psychology* 75(2):561-574.

DiBartolo, M. C. 2006. Careful hand feeding: A reasonable alternative to PEG tube placement in individuals with dementia. *Journal of Gerontological Nursing* 32(5):25-33.

Dollard, J., L. W. Doob, N. E. Miller, O. H. Mowrer, and R. R. Sears. 1939. *Frustration and Aggression*. New Haven: Yale University.

Duval, T. S., P. J. Silvia, and N. Lalwani. 2001. *Self-Awareness and Causal Attribution: A Dual-Systems Theory*. Boston: Klewer.

Emmons, R. A., and M. E. McCullough. 2003. Counting blessings versus burdens: An experimental investigation of gratitude and subjective well-being in daily life. *Journal of Personality and Social Psychology* 84(2): 377-389.

Epstein, R. 2001. The prince of reason: An interview with Albert Ellis. *Psychology Today* 31(1):66-68, 70-72, 74-76.

Finucane, T. E., C. Christmas, and K. Travis. 1999. Tube feeding in patients with advanced dementia: A review of the evidence. *Journal of the American Medical Association* 282(14):1365-1370.

Fisher, E. S., D. E. Wennberg, T. A. Stukel, D. J. Gottlieb, F. L. Lucas, and E. L. Pinder. 2003. The implications of regional variations in Medicare spending. Part 2: Health outcomes and satisfaction with care. *Annals of Internal Medicine* 138(4):288-298.

Frecska, E., and Z. Kulcsar. 1989. Social bonding in the modulation of the physiology of ritual trance. *Ethos* 17(1):70-87.

Hallenbeck, J. L. 2003. *Palliative Care Perspectives.* New York: Oxford University Press.

Horney, K. 1950. *Neurosis and Human Growth: The Struggle Toward Self-Realization.* New York: Norton.

Janoff-Bulman, R. 1992. *Shattered Assumptions: Towards a New Psychology of Trauma.* New York: Free Press.

Kübler-Ross, E. 1969. *On Death and Dying.* New York: Macmillan.

Larson, D. G. 1993. *The Helper's Journey: Working with People Facing Grief, Loss, and Life-Threatening Illness.* Champaign, IL: Research Press.

Lattanzi-Licht, M., J. J. Mahoney, and G. W. Miller. 1998. *The Hospice Choice: In Pursuit of a Peaceful Death.* New York: Fireside.

Lawler, K. A., J. W. Younger, R. L. Piferi, E. Billington, R. Jobe, K. Edmondson, and W. H. Jones. 2003. A change of heart: Cardiovascular correlates of forgiveness in response to interpersonal conflict. *Journal of Behavioral Medicine* 26(5):373-393.

Lehman, D. R., J. H. Ellard, and C. B. Wortman. 1986. Social support for the bereaved: Recipients' and providers' perspectives on what is helpful. *Journal of Consulting and Clinical Psychology* 54:438-446.

Lerner, E. B., D. V. Jehle, D. M. Janicke, and R. M. Moscati. 2000. Medical communication: Do our patients understand? *American Journal of Emergency Medicine* 18(7):764-766.

Lerner, M. J. 1980. *The Belief in a Just World: A Fundamental Delusion.* New York: Plenum Press.

Morris, V. 2004. *How to Care for Aging Parents.* New York: Workman.

Serrano, J. P., J. M. Latorre, M. Gatz, and J. Montanes. 2004. Life review therapy using autobiographical retrieval practice for older adults with depressive symptomatology. *Psychology and Aging* 19(2):272-277.

Snyder, C. R. 1994. *The Psychology of Hope: You Can Get There From Here.* New York: Free Press.

Spiegel, D. 1995. *Living Beyond Limits: New Hope and Healing for Facing Life-Threatening Illness.* New York: Random House.

Tedeschi, R. G., and L. G. Calhoun. 1996. The Posttraumatic Growth Inventory: Measuring the positive legacy of trauma. *Journal of Traumatic Stress* 9(3):455-471.

Teno, J. M. 2001. Brown atlas of dying. Retrieved March 23, 2007, from the Facts on Dying database, www.chcr.brown.edu/dying/BROWNATLAS.HTM.

Vachon, M. L., A. R. Sheldon, W. J. Lancee, W. A. Lyall, J. Rogers, and S. J. Freeman. 1982. Correlates of enduring distress patterns following bereavement: Social network, life situation, and personality. *Psychological Medicine* 12(4):783-788.

Weissman, D. E. 2003. Brain failure: A new diagnosis in palliative care. *Journal of Palliative Medicine* 6(3):335-336.

Wells, T., S. Falk, and P. Dieppe. 2004. The patients' written word: A simple communication aid. *Patient Education and Counseling* 54(2):197-200.

Yamhure-Thompson, L., C. R. Snyder, L. Hoffman, S. T. Michael, H. N. Rasmussen, L. S. Billings, L. Heinze, J. E. Neufeld, H. S. Shorey, J. C. Roberts, and D. E. Roberts. 2005. Dispositional forgiveness of self, others, and situations. *Journal of Personality* 73(2):313-359.

David B. Feldman, Ph.D, is assistant professor of counseling psychology at Santa Clara University. He holds a Ph.D. in clinical psychology from the University of Kansas and completed a fellowship in palliative care at the VA Palo Alto Health Care System, where he worked with countless patients and families confronting serious medical illness. His research and writings have addressed such topics as hope, meaning, and growth in the face of life's difficult circumstances.

Steven Andrew Lasher, Jr., MD, is currently director of palliative medicine at California Pacific Medical Center in San Francisco, CA. He also serves as the San Francisco medical director of Sutter Visiting Nurses Association Hospice and Home Care as well as the medical director of Coming Home Hospice. He completed his residency in internal medicine at Stanford Hospital and Clinics in Palo Alto, CA, as well as fellowship training in palliative medicine at Stanford/Palo Alto Veteran's Hospital.

Foreword writer **Ira Byock, MD,** is author *Dying Well* and *The Four Things That Matter Most.*

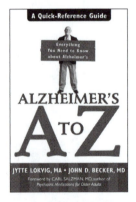
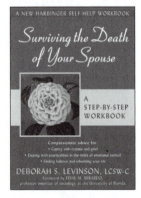